Content

A Note from the Author

A Word about Process

Part One: How Firm a Foundation
    Opening the Door
    Getting Grounded (Literally and Spiritually)
    Finding the One

Part Two: Rock of Ages
    Newlyweds
    Building a Family
    Location, Location, Location

Another Note from the Author

Part Three: On Shaky Ground
    Kawasaki Baby
    RAD, Really RAD
    The Business of Church
    Sabbatical

Part Four: Sinking Sand
    Yahweh Unraveled
    Amendment One Undone
    Two Paths, One Journey
    Get a Job

Part Five: Climbing Out
    The Santa Claus Effect
    WWJD (or What with Jesus Do)?
    Getting a Foothold

A Note from the Author

If faith is, as the Bible suggests, the "substance of things hoped for, the evidence of things unseen," then by that standard, I am a woman of great faith. I have faith that my children will grow up to lead full lives and that my husband and I will grow old together. I carry hope that humanity will evolve toward greater equality, greater compassion for all living creatures, and greater consideration for the earth's resources and our use of them. I have faith in the universe to sustain herself by creating mindfulness in her human trustees. I believe these things will come to pass, even if not in my lifetime. I hope for these things. I have tremendous faith.

If, however, you regard faith in the context of the prominent contemporary Christian belief system as defined by acknowledgement and reverence to one God - that being Yahweh of the Old Testament and the incarnate Jesus of the New Testament - then I am sorely lacking and surely fallen from grace.

Of course, to say that I have fallen implies that I at one time had a decent footing. And so I did. The latter described faith was both my foundation and the measure of my whole being from the time I was a child, specifically from my conversion at eight years old until some thirty years later when that foundation began crumbling beneath me.

My journey as it's recorded here is not meant to be prescriptive as much as introspective. I am writing it first and foremost for me: to remember, to examine, to confirm. How others may receive it I cannot control.

Living in close proximity to a Baptist seminary (and having lived long within the sphere of its teaching), I know that some of you will read this simply to find its flaws. You'll look for every opportunity to discredit my logic, to question my understanding of scripture, or to raise suspicion over my intentions. And if all else fails, you'll ignore the historical evidence, the testimony of witnesses, and my own personal experience and write me off as one who was never counted among the true believers. You will judge me in stark contradiction to your very own defenses and will turn a blind eye to the inconsistency. So be it.

But some of you will read it and see yourself along the path, your own doubts coming to light. It's not my desire to evangelize you to unbelief. But maybe like me, you have harbored those uncertainties in a very deep and lonely place. In that case, it is my sincere hope to inform you that you are not alone. Your questions are legitimate and worth asking and the range of acceptable answers may look very different for you.

Whatever your motivation for choosing this book – to scoff, to refute, to explore, to embrace, to balance the night stand in your guest room, whatever – I'm grateful for your willingness to share my journey.

A Word about Process

I'm guessing we've all seen a movie in which the perfect couple, having been ripped apart by some dastardly villain's schemes, is finally reunited. The estranged lover begins the harrowing tale of his journey back to her arms but she stops him with a passionate kiss and declares, "All that matters is that you're here now!" Do you find yourself thinking, as I do, that the body count and the continuous stream of seductresses he encountered along the way would be useful information?

In the real world, *process* can be as important as the finished product. It matters as much *how* we arrived as *that* we arrived. Just ask Lance Armstrong, recently stripped of his Tour de France titles for doping. Process counts.

Throughout my own transition process of reading, hearing other de-conversion stories, and engaging with many Christians I have concluded that skepticism like ours is usually dismissed in one of three ways.

- Simplifying the intellectual search

    On more than one occasion it has been suggested that my husband and I simply "read too much." People who have spent years and thousands of dollars on seminary education or have invested lifelong involvement in Sunday school, discipleship courses, and personal study have ironically cited the pursuit of knowledge as our downfall. Their premise must be that we formulated certain presuppositions about the faith and sought only texts which would confirm our suspicions. On the contrary, our reading list (as well as documentaries, podcasts, debates, etc.) was vast and varied. We would have welcomed an author who could satisfy our concerns and restore the foundational basis for our lives up to this point. We would have gladly returned to "business as usual" and avoided the excruciating emotional upheaval. No such luck.

- Simplifying the circumstances

Burn out, fatigue, stress, frustration, disappointment or any combination of these is enough to make someone struggle with doubt, right? To be sure. But they cannot be isolated as the sole cause for apostasy unless one is willing (and most Christians are not) to concede that belief is also purely circumstantial. In truth, no person or resulting decision is autonomous. We are each the sum of many parts, thoroughly homogenized. Therefore, it's illogical to make a singular argument either for or against belief based on external circumstances alone. It is however, both plausible and necessary that they be incorporated into the whole. In this book I will try to present my experiences as they are – highly influential but none independently blameworthy.

- Simplifying the motivation

I do not think, unless it has been said out of our hearing, that we have been accused of any great immorality apart from disbelief itself. But it's not uncommon and I won't be surprised when it happens. One pastor we served under made it a frequent sermon note that those who abandon the faith do so "in order to justify their sinful desires, addictions, or adulterous affairs." Well, as of this writing my and Tim's marriage is twenty years strong and in many ways, better than ever. Addictions? Not so much. While we enjoy a good beer, glass of wine, Pina Colada on occasion neither of us has ever been drunk. No illicit drugs, either. So, aside from my previously existing desire to get a tattoo and to go dancing at a gay/lesbian club (I've been assured they have the best music), there's not much we are doing now that we wouldn't have done before. Not to mention that we were in some sense at the height of ministry when all of this hit. There was no self-satisfying reason for turning our family, finances and future completely upside-down. As I said before, if given a sufficient "out" we would have taken it.

It's in response to these and with respect to process that I'm including a lengthy section on my life as a Christian and at the risk of really confusing things, I will share the story just as I lived it - fully trusting, fully invested. I won't autocorrect with "used to think" or "back when I believed" because it would not be true to my experience. I know that some will insist on discrediting thirty plus years of my life but I refuse to make it easy for them. And so we begin…

Part One: How Firm a Foundation

"Behold, I stand at the door and knock. If anyone hears my voice and opens the door, I will come in to him, and dine with him, and he with me." Revelation 3:20

Opening the Door

I loved Jesus. I didn't fully understand why. I never thought to question it. It just was. I loved him without any need for explanation in the same way I loved my parents and grandparents. All were part of my life from the very beginning - the latter in a tangible sense, the former otherwise invisible but an undeniable constant.

In the front bedroom of my grandmother's house hung a large portrait – a common depiction of Jesus knocking on a wooden door. On countless occasions, most often when I was supposed to be napping, I would lie on the bed staring up at that painting. Tender-heart that I was, it drew intense sadness from me. I couldn't imagine how anyone could leave this man out in the cold. I would gaze at his gentle face and mesmerizing (though woefully inaccurate) blue eyes trying to communicate through mental telepathy. "I'd open that door for you," I would think again and again.

Sometimes I'd imagine myself inside the picture, swinging the door open wide. Jesus would come in and warm himself by the fire and we'd sit there in peaceful silence. The thought brought satisfaction deep in my gut. This two-dimensional Jesus was the "lover of my soul" long before I knew what lover meant.

To say that I was raised in church would be an understatement. Church was life and Jesus was the life of the church as far as I was concerned. I sang "Oh, How I Love Jesus" with full gusto - the "oh, how" implicit with devotion. The life of Christ, His kindness to strangers and hands-on compassion, resonated with my empathetic nature.

I was the kid who was perpetually "rescuing" stray or wounded animals. I saw the best in everyone, even at their worst. My mother had to be called to school often when my first grade teacher was at a loss for what to do with a child who cried every time another student was punished. Fairly administered consequence or not, I hated seeing anyone/anything suffer.

In seventh grade I provided quite the entertainment for my youth pastor when he beheaded a snake during a lake retreat despite my sobbing pleas for its release. I should mention that the snake was venomous and posed an actual threat to our safety. I don't claim to have been rational, only compassionate. I ignored the leader's teasing references to Jesus "crushing the head of the serpent" and reinforced my own notion that if Jesus had been there, he would've been my advocate in the cause. In a sense, I was asking "what would Jesus do?" before it was marketable.

And I think it goes without saying but I didn't need the extremes of Mel Gibson's cinematographers to weep over the crucifixion. The King James Bible's rendering was enough. It broke my heart that one man would suffer punishment for everyone else's issues. The depth of the word injustice was not in my grasp at that age but I knew what was fair and what was not, and this was not fair!

I would have that same feeling again years later, in eighth grade, after watching "Ghandi." And then again while studying the life and death of Martin Luther King, Jr. To this day, I am accused of having an "overdeveloped sense of justice." I take it as a compliment.

But with Jesus, there was something different – personal and painfully clear when I was eight years old. It was my fault that Jesus died. He died because of me. My sins. This understanding devastated me and found me stumbling to the altar of my church, begging for forgiveness and a chance to spend my life making it up to him.

I was baptized that night wearing a white robe. The water was lukewarm. The preacher's hair was perfect. I had never really examined him this closely. He was wearing a dress shirt and tie under his robe and I wondered how he was keeping it dry. I never learned his secret but as an adult, my husband served under a pastor who made good use of his fishing waders during baptisms. Of course, today many churches use cleverly designed pools with a "dry area" so that pastors only need to roll up their sleeves.

The baptismal backdrop was a hand-painted mural of a bubbling stream that seemed to flow right into the very water I was standing in. There were several words spoken but I was intently listening for my cue: "In the name of the Father, Son, and Holy Spirit." I drew a quick breath. The pastor placed a small cloth over my mouth and nose and down I went. "Buried in the likeness of Christ. Raised to walk in the newness of life."

Nothing magical happened, nor did I expect it to. I went in dry, came out wet. But I did *feel* different. "To walk in newness of life" meant I was on my way to repaying the debt. It was very clear to me that salvation was a free gift, impossible to earn, but this was a debt of gratitude. I had opened the door and Jesus was there sitting by the fire. I was determined to fervently stoke that fire, not to keep him there but to make him smile. It was the least I could do.

Again, this was a very natural reaction for me. I remember once when my mother had to convince me that it was unnecessary to send a "thank you" note in response to someone else's thank you note. A perpetual cycle of kind words and affirmation made perfect sense to me.

Getting Grounded (Literally and Spiritually)

Life moved along in fairly predictable routines. We were a pretty typical Christian family: spit-shined with ties on the boys and pantyhose on the girls every Sunday morning. We had Sunday dinner with the grandparents, took an afternoon nap, and then headed back in time for "training union" and evening services. Wednesday nights were G.A.'s (Girls in Action) then eventually youth group meetings.

Seventh grade was a pivotal time for me. Our church had experienced some staff transitioning which meant that the new youth pastor and his wife made their first appearance the same day I did – promotion Sunday, early summer, 1986. I was twelve years old and sweating bullets because I was so nervous. Wesley was sweating through his perfectly starched white shirt because he was so nervous. Debbie wore wide-framed glasses atop a slightly pointed nose and had a gap between her front teeth just like mine. I fell in love with them instantly.

When he wasn't trying to corral crazy teenagers, Wes was a firefighter. He worked a standard twenty-four hours on, forty-eight hours off. Most of those working shifts, I could be found hanging out with Debbie. I would sleep over and we would stay up late talking about everything under the sun. I wasn't like many kids I knew who couldn't talk to their moms. My mom was accessible, just distracted. She and my dad had their hands full with my fifteen year-old sister and her personal rebellion. So it was good to have someone to bounce things off of and those midnight sessions did a great deal to anchor my faith.

That's not to say that I didn't have my share of typical teenage struggles. There was a brief period in the summer between seventh and eighth grade when I tried smoking. I was never really successful but I did try and that included swiping a few cigs from my dad while no one was looking. But my conscience wouldn't let me off so easy. The night came when I couldn't sleep, my guilt was so heavy. I prayed and prayed, cried and cried, repented again and again. I knew I would never do it again and somewhere around five in the morning I finally found sleep.

I woke up feeling clean and refreshed and ready to put it behind me, right up until my sister and I got into a fight.

She was more than sick of being the "trouble maker" in the house and threatened to out me to our parents. I told her about the long night of prayerful self-loathing and my resolve to end the deception. I'll never forget the look on her face. "What-the-hell-ever!" comes close. No doubt she thought I was looking for a "get out of jail free" card and there was no way she was letting this chance go. She told. And although my dad admitted he couldn't rightly punish me for something he'd been my primary example of, he did warn me of the natural consequences of addictions and then grounded me for lying and sneaking around.

The worst trouble of my life also came that tumultuous thirteenth year. A girlfriend was staying over on a Saturday night and we had asked to meet a couple more friends, uh, boys that is, at the mall, and had been firmly denied permission. We were to stay home and watch movies while my parents went out for the evening. Maybe it was classic peer pressure. Maybe it was hormones. Maybe I just figured a kid as compliant as I *usually* was deserved a "yes." Whatever the reason, we concocted a plan to get out and get back without my parents knowing. It was a brilliant plan for an utterly stupid idea.

I won't bother with the full details. Suffice it to say two thirteen year old girls out with five guys ranging from thirteen to seventeen (none of whom I'd ever laid eyes on before) on the back side of a neighboring town (where I'd never been before) *could* have been disastrous. In retrospect, I think *stupid, stupid, stupid.* We had no money, no such thing as a cell phone, no idea where we were, and of course, no one else who knew where we were either.

Did I mention *stupid, stupid, stupid*? But if that wasn't bad enough, our self-appointed curfew (aka sneak back in before mom and dad get home time) came...and went.

I won't lie to you. I was having fun. And once you got past the overarching deception of it all, we weren't doing anything bad, just hanging out. I'd seen my sister pull this type of stunt dozens of times. There would be a fight, plenty of yelling, and she'd be grounded for a week or two but by then, the fun was had. From my perspective, the experience was worth the backlash this one time. It stopped being worth it as soon as we arrived home and my sister informed me our parents were at the police station filing a "missing persons" report. It was nearing one in the morning.

My friend's father picked her up and encouraged us to "Say your goodbyes. You won't be seeing each other for a very long time." Three hours of interrogation and lecturing later, my sister (whose last words to me that night were "I don't care what you do just leave my name out of it!" Again –sorry about that, Terrie.) and I were sent to bed. Our official sentencing would fall after church services the next day, giving us time to "think about what you've done" and my folks time to cool off. It was the most torturous day of my life - which I truly believed was over. They'd probably never let me get a driver's license, and dating? Forget it! My first date would be my wedding day, if anyone would have me after years of solitary confinement.

Despite their clear disappointment in our behavior, my youth pastor and his wife spoke out on our behalf. Wesley went to my parents saying, "They are your girls to do with as you see fit but I truly believe there is no punishment you can give them that will be worse than the anxiety they are feeling while waiting for it." It was true and my parents were gracious. In the end we were given one consequence: apologize and ask for forgiveness. Seems simple enough but I'm embarrassed to say it took me hours to act on it. Pride? Sure. Embarrassment? Heck yeah. Stubborness? Am I my father's child? (That would be a "yes"). All of the above? Absolutely!

So, I wasn't perfect, but all in all, I leaned way farther to the "goodie-two-shoes" side of life than the "rebel-without-a-cause." And while I was far from an evangelist those middle and high school years, I was very open regarding my faith and held firm to my convictions. I was easily guilt-ridden, grieved heavily over my own sins, and was sincerely bothered by the hypocrisy of other Christians. Still, my compassionate side tended to keep hyper-judgments at bay and allowed me a wide range of relationships and more than a few unlikely friendships.

In ninth grade I learned the ultimate lesson in unexpected friendship and not "judging a book by its cover." I began a new school that year, out of my usual district. I knew no one. Not a soul. Those first few days of school were excruciating. I paid attention to mannerisms and eaves-dropped on conversations to identify the typical church kids, assuming that's where I'd fit in. I attempted a few exchanges but to no avail. Mostly I felt like a shadow, moving from class to class unnoticed.

On the fourth day, I put on my brave face and again, sat alone at the end of a lunch table, staring at my tray and choking down dry French-fries. A voice saying "hey" brought my head up. I was looking into the face of a girl who was nothing if not my complete opposite. I was tall and lanky with red hair. She was short and a bit pudgy with hair dyed jet black. It was cut very short except for her bangs, which were spiked straight up in the front. Of course, it was the eighties so the bangs were not *that* shocking. I was wearing pin-striped slacks and a pastel peach sweater with beige flats. She was wearing a solid black shift dress with black leggings and huge men's combat boots. Her fingernail polish and eye make-up were as black as her hair. She wore skull-faced rings on several fingers and in contrast to everything else her lips were crimson red.

"We noticed you sit by yourself. Do you want to sit with us?" she asked and motioned a few tables over.

There was a whole table of... *them*. They were skaters, punks, Goths, and various combinations of the three, but at that moment they looked more like Jesus to me than the Christian kids. I scooped up my tray and joined them. They talked of half-pipes, the Sex Pistols, and zombies (way before zombies were cool). Their ambassador of peace who'd rescued me from my solitude, Lillian, was the most confident, self-assured girl I'd ever met, and we instantly became best friends.

My high school years were characterized by interactions like this. Geeks, jocks, potheads, Goths, cheerleaders, lesbians, disabled, black, white, Hispanic... labels just never meant much to me. As far as I was concerned, every other effort to be Christ-like could fail miserably but loving people was not optional. It was what Jesus did so, it was what I did.

Finding the One

My junior year of high school I fell in love. Tim and I met the year before during a performance of "Into the Woods," so it can't technically be called love at first sight. We were both dating other people, but he definitely caught my attention. During one rehearsal I pointed him out to my mom and said, "I want to take him home, set him on my dresser, and have him sing me to sleep every night." He had the most beautiful voice.

It wasn't until the next year when we were cast opposite each other as Tony and Maria in a production of "West Side Story" that the full picture came into view. I knew early on that Tim was the one. He was openly Christian, unbelievably talented, and crazy handsome to boot. But we had a rocky start due to some experiences (not my stories to share) that left me disillusioned and fearful of relationship. Tim broke up with me a couple of times because he felt I was sending him "mixed signals" and given my timidity, I've no doubt that's exactly what I was doing. But all in all, we were inseparable. Until we faced the biggest hurdle of our dating relationship: Tim decided to attend a Christian liberal arts school in the tiny town of Anderson, Indiana. You know, the Indiana that is approximately six hundred miles from my home in Atlanta, Georgia. We dreaded the ups and downs of a long-distance relationship for a year…then came a small miracle.

My dad worked for General Motors, which meant he spent much time laid off or on union strike. Such was the case at the end of my junior year as Tim's departure grew closer, only this time the plant was closing and relocation was inevitable. Every few weeks dad would receive an "option letter," naming the location of another plant for him to consider. The places were spread all over the country and there was one catch: at some point and without notice, options would run out and an "assignment letter" would be issued instead. It was an anxious time for the whole family until one day when dad opened the mail and with a half-laugh, half-moan, passed a letter to me. I scanned to the middle of the page and stared in disbelief at the words "Anderson, Indiana." I'm pretty sure I screamed.

"Daddy!" I exclaimed. "It's God's will for us to move to Indiana so that Tim and I can be together!"

What were the odds? Really? It all made perfect sense to me. My dad and Tim would be able to keep each other company and my mom, brother, and I would stay in Georgia while I finished out my senior year without changing schools. Then we'd all be together the following year. Miracle number two: my parents agreed.

Now, if you ask them, they will tell you that they weighed out the pros and cons and made the decision based on practicality and logic. *Logic shmogic.* As far as I was concerned, God was moving mountains (at least the Harrington family) so that His will for my and Tim's future together would be accomplished. It was all about me. Obviously.

The year progressed. Tim and Dad bonded over pizza, the Atlanta Braves, and homesickness. Mom and I kept the roads hot visiting as often as possible. It was a long year for all of us but my high school graduation soon came and the moving plans were being finalized. I'd been accepted to the same college and had a dorm assignment. My future roommate was traveling all the way from California. I couldn't believe it was really happening. Tim was home for the summer and we would never have to be apart again.

And then...Tim received a letter in the mail from the university. It seemed he'd miscalculated the GPA requirement for one of his two scholarships and would no longer be receiving a certain portion of those funds. In short, this meant that Tim's career at this college had just come to an abrupt end. I was shocked. Devastated. For the life of me, I could not figure out what God was thinking. I went to my parents, again, and made a tearful plea.

"I think it's God's will for me to stay here and live with my grandparents so that Tim and I can be together."

Let me interject something here: my parents have never been wealthy. Heck, they would barely qualify as well-off. They scrape by and that's that. In retrospect, I have no idea how my parents intended to pay the tuition for a school that Tim's family, who were much more financially stable, could not afford to pay even with one scholarship still available. And while I'm certain they struggled with the idea of leaving me behind, this had to have been a relief in light of the exorbitant debt they were looking to rack up on my education. So, miracle number three: they conceded to let me live with my grandparents and attend community college while the rest of the family moved north.

A year later, on my nineteenth birthday, Tim asked me to marry him. It was picturesque and perfect, if you don't count the fact that Tim stalled until the last possible moment of our date and that I was in tears having suspected and subsequently given up on the proposal, thanks to said stalling. Timing aside, he asked, I said yes, we were happy. Another year and two months later we were married. Despite almost four years of dating, Tim and I were both virgins on our wedding day. We believed God's word and while we can't claim total innocence in the matter, we did fight temptation to maintain the basic standard set by scripture. It was important to us that this be a testimony of God at work in us during our wedding ceremony, which prompted a decision I have regretted for many years.

In January, six months prior to our wedding date, my unmarried sister discovered that she was pregnant. I did the math and given her tiny frame, realized that her "condition" would be quite visible by the day of our ceremony. I was afraid that the gossip over her clearly noticeable indiscretion would overshadow the sexual integrity Tim and I hoped to portray in our union. And so, I asked her to not to be in my wedding party. She was hurt. Angry. But my conviction wouldn't allow me to forfeit my testimony.

Our wedding was beautiful. It went off without a hitch. It was Christ-centered, God was glorified, and the gospel was evident. *But* if you (reader) will indulge me one moment…

An Open Letter to My Sister,

If I could go back, there are probably many things I would change –the horrendous bridesmaids' dresses, maybe the way I wore my hair. But nothing more important than this: to have you standing by my side, holding my bouquet, and yes, even balancing the round belly you were sporting to straighten the hem of my dress. Not one of the ladies lined along the stairs that day had shared my conviction of saving sex for marriage - not one. But theirs was a "sin" unseen and somehow I allowed that to justify my choice. I was wrong. It is that simple. I don't know if Tim and I will ever get or take the opportunity to renew our wedding vows but if so, I hope you will allow me to redeem myself and that you'd be willing to take a place of honor beside me – right where you should have been that June day so many years ago. I love you!

Part Two: Rock of Ages

"My hope is built on nothing less than Jesus blood and righteousness."

-Edward Mote

Newlyweds

Our lives revolved around two things: work and church. Already, Tim had the desire to be in ministry full-time and transferred his college credits to Luther Rice Bible College where he both attended and completed "external" courses at home. We were both working secular jobs to make ends meet when Tim came across a listing for a music director/youth pastor position in central Georgia. We drove down for an interview with the "search committee" on a Wednesday afternoon. We made our way through a couple of tiny towns including Monticello, home of famous country singer Trisha Yearwood, and then along Highway 212. At that time it was an 30-minute stretch of nothing but trees on both sides - a sleepy drive to say the least. Tim directed a choir rehearsal and then we were invited back the following Sunday to meet the youth and for Tim to direct Sunday morning worship. The congregation voted immediately after the service and we were welcomed to the family with an *almost* unanimous vote. Not sure who the hold-out was, but we were told this person voted against everything so not to take it personally.

We packed up our lives and moved to an apartment in Milledgeville, Georgia. We couldn't afford to live in the community where the church was located. Pretty much all of the houses were lakeside or lake view properties and we were first time home buyers and still newlyweds with no savings to speak of. We eventually purchased a home in a neighboring town. I loved the little house but hated the eighteen-mile one way commute that Tim had to make four days a week, twice on Wednesdays, four times on Sundays, and multiple times on weekends for youth activities. He was basically being paid to keep gas in the car.

I worked full-time at The Animal Hospital of Milledgeville as a receptionist and assistant when needed. Favorite. Job. Ever. I loved the animals, always had, but I also loved the people with and for whom I worked. Dr. Lee was "old money" and had his place among the elite of historical Milledgeville. His and his first wife's home had been featured once in Southern Living Magazine. Unfortunately, she committed suicide shortly after. I never probed for the details of her death and it was not something Dr. Lee spoke of often but I remember one day as I shared anxiety over some circumstance in my life, he quietly described walking into his house that day and finding her body. He looked at me with moist eyes and said, "You never know what you are strong enough to handle until you *have* to be strong enough." I always thought it was this part of his life that made him seem down to earth and approachable despite his wealth and prominence in the community.

Dr. Council was something of an alter-ego to Dr. Lee. For starters, Dr. C was female and a healthy feminist at that. She was determined to make her own place in the community and it would not be as the prim southern arm-piece to any man. Her husband owned and operated a salon in town but she was fiercely independent, determined to prove herself and quite capable.

She was my employer first and foremost but I also considered her a friend. We shared many ideas, including our faith. She was, however, Pentecostal, which led to countless debates over issues of eternal security, baptism of the Holy Spirit, and the sign gifts in general. In retrospect, she was my first real exposure to Pervasive Interpretive Pluralism (more in later chapters) before I knew what it was. I just thought she was wrong. Plain wrong because nothing in my experience confirmed her interpretation of Scripture and all of the Baptist teaching I'd received thoroughly denied her experience. In the end, we agreed to disagree and rested on what we had in common.

Derrick and Tyrone were the guys who worked in the back and assisted with exams and surgeries. They were a constant source of entertainment. Derrick had worked for Dr. Lee the longest of all of us and there was nothing (short of operating and I'm almost convinced he could've done that, too) that he could not do. It was a great atmosphere - stressful at times, but almost always full of teasing and laughter.

When I wasn't working, I was helping Tim and hanging out with teenagers. I had stepped into the role that Wesley and Debbie had played for me years before and like them, I had a constant stream of kids running through my living room. I lived in a perpetual state of exhaustion but it was also fulfilling. I was writing skits and Bible studies, teaching, singing, and using my creative gifts in myriad ways.

I was also volunteering at a crisis pregnancy center in town thanks to the urging of my husband and the center's director, Judy Butler. They met once when Tim was collecting brochures for our "True Love Waits" campaign. Judy had been lovingly nagging Tim to send me her way for months before I actually made an appearance. Judy was a fabulous woman. She was full of compassion for both unborn babies *and* the women who carried them - a rare combination in those days - but she also had a fire behind her eyes and a load of tenacity. She had fought through breast cancer using alternative treatments and an organic diet. I adored her and hold her responsible in many ways for my family as it exists now. It was during my time at the clinic that I was most surprised by the reality of hypocrisy I encountered, some within the church and some within myself.

Year after year, Judy appealed to the local churches for funds and year after year, the budget was barely met by the same faithful contributors. The church just couldn't shake the notion that unplanned pregnancy was a "them" problem. You know…them, the outsiders, the non-believers, the un-churched. Problem was, I filed the paperwork. Almost every girl, at least 90%, claimed membership in a church within 20 miles of the center. Even if you made allowance for non-attending members, backsliders, and outright liars, it would still easily account for more than half. Based on the financial support, you might have been tempted to think that abstinence was the rule among church kids. You'd have been so very wrong.

On a personal level, I was successfully running my own scam job. Day after day, I would meet with girls whose lives were upside down. I would try to convince them that God was the creator of life and that children, all children, had inherent value to Him. Because of that they should, at the very least, cry out to Him for help before making a decision they would live with the rest of their lives. Meanwhile, ironically, I was popping birth control having never even considered it a matter of prayer, just pragmatism. You get married, you go on the pill, and then you have a baby when you decide you're ready. Tim and I would be meandering through the grocery store and when we got to the baby items aisle one of us would inevitably comment: "Thank God we don't need any of that stuff!" And of course, there were those times when I'd forget to take the pill and have to double up, causing us to wait anxiously, breathing a sigh of relief when my period would come because it was just "not a good time" for us to have a baby.

Then one day, sitting in the center office, a terrible conviction washed over me. I assumed I would never abort a baby but I suddenly realized that my attitude toward children was no different than the girls I was counseling. Children were an afterthought at best and an inconvenience to be avoided. What right did I have to tell anyone to trust God in the midst of an unplanned pregnancy when I had never given Him so much as an honorable mention in regard to my own reproductive health? It would be comical if it were not so disparate: a twenty-three year old woman with a husband, a home, and two full-time incomes who panics over a late period trying to convince a seventeen year old girl not to freak out and do something rash.

I went home and shared my thoughts with Tim. I remember him holding his hand up at one point and saying, "I'm going to need a moment to process this." Then, he did what my husband had always done in the face of new information: he searched the scripture. Within two days, he'd compiled a list of verses regarding children. He came to me and said, "You're right. We don't love children the way God does. We have to change."

I stopped taking birth control. It was scary but the alternative felt like less than obedience and less than the reflection of God's image we hoped to represent. There was (is) a popular justification among young couples that "If God wants us to get pregnant, we have faith that He can make it happen even if we're using birth control." Sounds great, doesn't it? But it's just lip-service to God's sovereignty because as soon as we suggested that the natural inverse of this must be equally true: If God does *not* mean for you to be pregnant, He can prevent it *without* birth control," suddenly faith is usurped by almighty common sense.

Common sense is something we've been accused of lacking due to what we believed were biblical decisions. But we never assumed that following Christ would look or feel logical. On the contrary, we took the "Jesus Freak" label made popular by DC Talk to heart, and one of our favorite songs was Michael Card's "God's Own Fool," which portrays Christ as having been thought insane by his family and demonically oppressed by the religious sect. And who could possibly accuse the disciples, having left their livelihoods and loved ones to follow a penniless vagrant, of demonstrating common sense?

During the same time, Tim graduated from Bible college, was ordained as a minister, and felt "the call" to attend seminary. He'd narrowed it down to two campuses – Southeastern Baptist Theological Seminary in North Carolina or The Master's College in California. With this new prospect of moving, having a baby jumped from just a possibility to a serious priority. Sure, I was willing to trust God, but I wasn't all that keen on giving birth to my first child miles away from the one person who could help me through it. No, not Tim - my mom!

So, we started trying. And trying. And trying. Not that either of us were complaining about the effort, but needless to say, something wasn't working quite right. No pregnancy. Almost a year later and mere months before we would ship off to Tim's school of choice in NC, we sat down and talked through our options. Years earlier, still in our dating phase, I'd run across an article in the newspaper (you know, the primitive form of the internet) about a man who found an infant, a baby girl, abandoned in a train station in China. He paid three thousand dollars to the appropriate government officials and brought the child home to raise as his own. I was sixteen and had two immediate thoughts: 1–I have almost that much in my savings account from working a summer job, and 2–How is it possible that a child's life could be worth so little?

(Clearly, this took place before the explosion and subsequent regulation of international adoption.) I shared the story with Tim and told him that I intended to adopt someday and he should keep that in mind if he decided to marry me. This moment, along with my work in the pregnancy center, made adoption a natural part of our vocabulary.

Neither of us desired to be poked and prodded in search of the responsible party, and though many Christians come to a different conclusion, we could not justify spending as much or more money trying to "create" a child as it would take to provide a home for one that already existed. Again, scripture informed our process. The list of adopted characters from Moses all the way to Jesus himself was impressive. Add to that the doctrine of adoption as God's children and "joint heirs with Christ" and the evidence was overwhelming. "Children are a heritage from the Lord" and the fatherless were to be defended.

We located an agency and began the paperwork process. It was April –five months before we were scheduled to move out of state. I asked God for one thing…that our baby would arrive before we moved. I should've been more specific.

Building a Family

On August 10, 1999, exactly three days before moving, we drove to a small agency in south-central Georgia to pick up our "first-born" son. We were giddy with excitement and nerves. From that day forward, our lives would never be the same and that reality was wonderfully terrifying. Nathan was already five weeks old when we met him, but he'd been born six weeks premature and only weighed seven pounds, so he still felt awfully "new-born" to us. He was absolutely perfect and it took all of three seconds to fall madly in love with him - the exact time required to transfer him from the social worker's arms to mine.

My mom stayed with us the next two days as we acclimated to sleepless nights and packed up the few belongings that weren't already in storage. Then off we went with a small caravan of grandparents to Wake Forest, North Carolina and our new apartment home on seminary campus. I'll never forget that first day as neighbors welcomed us with helping hands. I desperately needed to direct the flow of boxes into the correct rooms, so I passed Nathan to the wife of one of the guys unloading the truck.

"What should I do if he gets fussy?" she asked with an edge of panic to her voice.

"I don't know. I've only had him three days, so let me know if you figure it out," I threw over my shoulder to her surprise.

Of course, we didn't have extensive training on the importance of bonding at this point or perhaps I would have done things differently. Our saving grace with Nathan was my attempt to nurse him using a Supplemental Nursing System which gave us lots of face time, and the fact that I was home with him every day, all day.

One of my greatest fears before adopting was that I would bring this child into my home and then regret it. My precious friend, Judy, from the crisis pregnancy center, encouraged me in that respect.

"There were days I wanted to take the children I gave birth to and throw them out of the nearest window," She assured me.

It was good to remember on days when nothing, absolutely nothing, would soothe that colicky little boy. While Nathan and I were developing a very strong bond, he was determined to test me in ways I'd never experienced. First, he insisted that he have my full attention every moment of the day. Laundry? Not unless he was sleeping. Dishes? Forget it. He would crawl between my legs and the sink cabinet and push with all his might to get me away from my task. He didn't necessarily want my participation; he would happily play with Matchbox cars for an hour as long as he had me as an audience. In retrospect, a kid who'd gone through four caregivers and three "homes" before he was two months old had every right to be insecure but at the time. But it was exhausting.

When he was around two, he had a series of night terrors. I'd never seen anything like this and honestly thought he was demonically oppressed (if not possessed) during the first episode. I heard a thump and when I checked on him, he was face-down on the floor. I was thinking *poor kid fell out of his toddler bed –no biggie*, but as I scooped him up he began thrashing and kicking me. The more I tried to soothe him the more violent he became. His eyes were as hard as glass and it was as though he was looking straight through me. Tim came in, hearing the commotion, and carried Nathan to our bed hoping he would settle down. It was a useless effort as he began hurling himself into our headboard. We stacked pillows behind him and stared helplessly. It was apparent that he was still in some stage of sleep and there were no other "medical" symptoms (fever, vomiting, etc). Without another obvious explanation, we did all we knew to do. Pray.

We contacted the "elder on call" at our church and asked him to come and pray over Nathan with us. I don't think he knew exactly what to do with this request, so first he gave us the emergency number for a local pediatrician to call and ask for advice. We tried - to no avail since we were not "established patients." By this time, the hour-plus of screaming and convulsing had subsided. Nathan was awake but groggy. We were still very shaken and still felt like prayer was in order and so, the elder came and prayed with us even though it was very late.

I spent the next day researching and learned about night terrors, which are much like nightmares only more physically dramatic. They occur as the child's brain is transitioning from non-REM to REM sleep, the same stage sleepwalking occurs. And while those of us who witness it come away traumatized, the child remembers nothing of it. Nathan had a few more episodes over the next months but none as severe as the first.

When night terrors weren't getting the best of him, he was creating daytime terror in his own special way: tantrums. One of my all-time favorite Nathan stories stems from his knack for throwing royal fits and pushing all of my buttons.

This particular day, the fit had quickly grown to all-out rage for both of us. In a moment of desperation, I attempted to restrain him and he, in turn, attempted to remove a chunk of my forearm with his teeth. I picked him up by the shoulders and deposited (dropped) him on his bed. Before closing the door, I growled through a clenched jaw "If you come out, I will kill you." (Proud parenting moment right there.) I grabbed the phone and called our church where Tim was on staff as a choir director.

After a few seconds on hold, Cindy, one of the church secretaries, came on the line and said, "Amie, we can't find Tim right now. Can I give him a message for you?"

A message indeed.

"Tell him that if he wants his son to live to see his third birthday, I need him to come home right now."

We hung up and within thirty seconds my phone rang.

"We haven't found Tim just yet, Amie but we're looking, okay?" Cindy explained.

"That's fine, Cindy." I tried to sound al little calmer than I had before. "It's just been a really rough morning."

Again we hung up, and again the phone rang just seconds later. This time it was the Pastor of Evangelism.

"Amie…everything okay over there?" He asked.

By this point, I'm not only furious with Nathan but I'm feeling very embarrassed. I tried again to explain that I was just having a bad day and needed to Tim to come home and give me a few minutes to catch my breath.

"Tell you what," he offered, "One of the secretaries and I will come and take Nathan off your hands for a few minutes until we can find Tim."

I felt stupid, but I'd already upset the entire office so I relented and hung up to wait for their arrival. Another ring of the phone and I answered it hesitantly. It was Cindy.

"Hey Amie. I'm just going to stay on the line with you until Pastor gets there, okay?" she said sweetly.

"Cindy" I sighed, "I wasn't actually going to kill him."

"I know. I know. You did the right thing by calling us," she assured me.

Well, now it was official. I'd jumped from stressed-out mom to mental health case. I imagined Cindy reading from an emergency response cue card with Paula, the church treasurer, listening in on another line for the sound of a shrieking child, fingers poised to dial 911. The pastor and secretary arrived - to my utter humiliation - followed shortly by Tim.

It's a funny story…now. More than once I made emergency calls to what I affectionately referred to as my "HIT Squad." That is: Homicide Intervention Team. (Yes, I realize team squad is redundant but just calling them "hit" was weird.) Anyway, if nothing else, Nathan Sexton taught me to laugh at myself since his antics required too many witnesses for straight-up denial and the alternative was to die of embarrassment.

We began the paperwork for our second adoption around the time Nathan was one. A few people thought we were crazy but unlike pregnancy, there's no standard gestational period for adoption and an unexpected hurdle can hold the process up indefinitely. We figured better sooner than later. Just over a year later, we found ourselves in another agency conference room awaiting our second son, Isaiah.

Three weeks earlier, the agency sent us a referral for a newborn, African-American boy. Nathan was bi-racial and often mistaken for Latino or Filipino, but this child was black. Just black. Whether or not you understand the nuances of race in this country, especially in the south (and there is not room in this book to explain it to you), please trust me when I say this was a big deal. We asked for the weekend to pray about it and get back to them.

A friend questioned me over lunch the next day.

"What is there to pray about?" she wondered.

I understood the nature of her question. We were in the "if God says it, we do it" camp, after all. But we also knew first hand that adoption is not (forgive the pun) a black-and-white issue. We'd seen and experienced things as Nathan's parents that most parents do not have to endure. We had supportive friends and family but there was no shortage of public opinion. Plenty of people openly displayed their disapproval with stares and hateful glares. But even well-meaning people revealed their ignorance and prejudice by their comments. Often (surprisingly often) we were asked about Nathan's ethnicity. When we explained that he was adopted domestically (not a "foreigner") and that he was mixed, black and white, their countenance would drop and they would shake their head in a piteous way and say "well, it's not *his* fault." The implication that someone must be "at fault" for a mixed-race child to exist left me biting my tongue and politely excusing myself from further conversation.

We had every reason to believe these incidents would not only continue but intensify with the adoption of a full African American child. So the time we spent praying that weekend was not meant to determine *if we should* welcome this child into our family but *if we were prepared* to and *capable* of instilling the confidence and security that this child would need to face these racial obstacles.

In the end, we decided that a good thing was a good thing even if it was hard and we sincerely believed that whatever we were lacking, Jesus would supply. So there we were again, picking up our three week old son. The doors opened and in walked the foster mom with the biggest newborn I had ever seen. Don't get me wrong, this child was embedded in my heart before I ever laid eyes on him. He was mine, all mine - from the top of his big-ass afro to the bottom of his ginormous feet - but to say I was taken aback is an understatement. Please remember that all we had to compare this moment to was his pint-sized premature "big brother." Isaiah had jumped from an average birth weight around eight pounds to a chart-topping twelve pounds in those first twenty-one days of life.

As she placed him in my arms, I hoped to God my smile was holding up. All I could think was *they have taken a seventy-five year old black woman and shrunk her down to a toddler sized baby boy. What am I supposed to do now?* On the way home, as baby boy nestled in his car seat (after the straps had to be adjusted for his surprisingly long body), Tim took me by the hand. "Whatcha thinking?" he asked. I smiled at him with tears stinging the backs of my eyes and said something to the effect of "I'm in love with the ugliest baby I've ever seen."

Tim let out a burst of laughter and said, "I am so glad *you* said it first!" Then we were both a mess of laughter and tears as we took that precious boy home and showed him off to everyone. Isaiah is still our gentle giant – a six foot tall, size thirteen shoe, twelve year old at this point –and still growing. And I must say, he is one handsome fellow, having grown into all his parts.

And yes, we have all endured our share of hurtful words, hateful looks, and unsolicited opinions, but that's how it goes with cross-racial adoption. Reactions run the gamut. At times we are the worst of sinners: stupid arrogant white people thinking we can raise a black child. Other times we are the rescuers of poor black children who otherwise were doomed to be gangsters, rapists, and prostitutes. We are saints but for all the wrong reasons. Throw in an adoption from Haiti (which you'll read more about in a later chapter) and we could easily be called everything from enablers to kidnappers to heroes. The truth is, we are not/were never any of those things. We were just people trying to be faithful to whatever God put in front of us.

Toward the end of 2006, it seemed He was determined to put us through the ringer. Tim was contacted by an adoption agency via a mutual friend. They'd learned that we had multiple children of minority races and asked if we'd consider adding another little bit of sunshine to our lives. Our youngest was almost six. We were a little freaked out but believed that "where God guides, He provides," so we agreed to start the paperwork, pray, and trust that whatever happened was His will.

Very shortly thereafter, we received a call and were invited to come and meet a young woman who was considering placement with us. It was a good meeting in whatever way it's "good" to have the difficult conversation with another woman about raising her child. It looked like things would move in the direction of her placing her child with us, a baby girl due in less than a month. We picked up a few baby items, starting to get very excited, and even picked out a name: Nakiah Journey Sexton. Nakiah meaning "faithful" and Journey meaning, well, "journey," but also in honor of Sojourner Truth, one of my personal heroines.

That's when things got crazy and my ovaries, who'd been useless up to this point in life, decided to become raging psychos. More specifically, I had an ovarian cyst which ruptured, landing me a day in the hospital and all kinds of uncertainty regarding my health. Blood work was drawn, tests were run, and I was panicking. Do we proceed with adoption plans? What if I have cancer? What if I die and leave Tim with not three, but four children? Over the next week, I waited anxiously. On Friday morning, a friend put me in contact with her OB/GYN who requested my file from the hospital but wouldn't get to review it until the following Monday. I just had to get through the weekend without losing my mind, and then at least, we would know.

Then came the call that I was not expecting. It was the agency. The baby girl had made an early appearance. She was fine but her birthmother had decided not to place after all. Suddenly, "our" baby was gone. We were heartbroken and torn. It is a complicated thing as an adoptive mom to mourn the loss of a child while equally supporting and even celebrating another woman's ability to care for her own child. It's this bizarre swirling of sorrow, guilt, admiration, and hope all blended up into a nauseating mess of emotion. In addition to all that, there was the "writing on the wall" regarding my health. I had cancer. It was the only thing that made sense. And in the weirdest way, this was my greatest relief. It answered the "why" question, and I really wanted an answer.

Cancer would be horrible, of course, but it allowed my mind to create a logical order of events. The adoption had required that I get a physical which included a routine pap smear. The Pap smear had irritated the ovarian cyst/cancer enough to create intense pain. The pain forced me to have tests run which would soon enough reveal the cancer. Having learned of the cancer, I would get the necessary treatments and in the end would give glory to God and gratitude for our would-be baby Nakiah for taking us on this "faithful journey." I had it all wrapped up with the bow on top.

Monday morning the doctor called. My blood work and the review of the ultrasound all indicated that I was cancer free. Free of cancer. Without cancer. Cancer-less. My world was shattered. I know exactly what you're thinking and you're absolutely right. Under any other circumstances this would have been the news I was begging God for but in this case, it just left me confused. I was more or less healthy. At least, I wasn't in imminent danger of death in which case, I had no idea why we had to go through the pain of expecting a baby girl and then losing her. What about the part where He "works all things together for my good?"

It took some time and more grieving but I eventually accepted that there didn't have to be a why, that it was more important to trust than to know. And while that sounds really good, I will say that looking back, it wasn't that trusting was a satisfactory answer, it was really just me creating a "greater good" within the act of yielding because I was never really content with a non-answer. I dare say none of us are, so we conjure purpose in abstract ideas such as obedience, faithfulness, submission, etc. to suffice until we can fill the gap with something more tangible.

For me, tangible peeked around the corner late one December night when Tim had a cough syrup/Holy Spirit induced epiphany.

Location, Location, Location

We were visiting family for Christmas vacation and poor Tim was suffering through his annual upper respiratory infection. In the middle of the night as he nursed his cough, he read through the blog of some of our dearest friends who were serving as full-time missionaries in Haiti. Next thing you know, he was emailing the director of their sponsoring organization and asking if they were in need of a second mission family. Of course, I knew nothing of this until the next morning as I was brushing my teeth and Tim peeked around the door and said sheepishly, "I should probably tell you what I've done."

This wasn't the first time we'd considered a move to Haiti. After many visits there over the course of adopting our daughter, we fell in love. It is one of the most beautifully desperate places and it easily climbs into your heart and takes root there.

Even when we knew service out of the country was not likely, we had pursued work with Haitian communities in the states. We interviewed with the North American Mission Board at one point in hopes of moving to Florida, Little Haiti to be exact, and planting a church or providing some other ministry. The interview was scheduled for one in the afternoon, just after lunch - clearly not a good call since the gentleman evaluating us continually nodded off over the course of a two hour Q & A. He would ask a question, we would proceed to answer, and within seconds his eyes would begin rolling to the back of his head. Fortunately for us (though unfortunately for them) he was accompanied by three young men who were in training for future positions within the organization so we simply directed most of our responses to them. Inevitably someone would clear their throat or the momentary silence would rattle the man from his slumber and he would throw out the next question and the cycle would repeat. It was incredibly awkward and embarrassing for all of us.

What was more awkward was when we got the summary of his evaluation in which he submitted to the Mission Board that were not quite ready for field work. "How the hell would he know?" I had exclaimed to Tim. Absurdity aside, the door had been closed so we moved on with life.

But this, this moment of Tim's Nyquil-buzzed inquiry was different than just a shot in the dark interview with Sleepy Dwarf. This was possible and all of the sudden it was very real and things were moving very fast. We made a trip to Kentucky to meet with the director of the organization and to see if we were a good match. There were red flags. Doctrinal red flags. Personality red flags. Eighties hairstyle red flags. And there were more and more "heads-ups" coming in from our friends already in Haiti regarding the leadership style of said director. This was hard for them and us. We all wanted to work together but they wanted us to come in with our eyes wide open. Ultimately, we knew we'd be serving with and have the support of our friends, living among people we'd grown to love, so we mentally notched everything down to *yellow* flags and continued moving forward. We prayed, we planned, we packed, we asked for pledges. We thought to ourselves how maybe, just maybe, the adoption falling through and the cancer scare had all been a test of sorts, a means of preparing us for the next crazy thing like moving to a third world country. Made sense, right? And then, on a Monday afternoon in early January, we answered the phone.

It was the adoption agency director. She wanted to know what we were up to. I was so surprised to hear from her because I'd made the assumption that adoption was off the "God's will" radar since Journey. I explained our current situation, the inevitable move, and that unless she had a baby who was already born and whose adoption could be completed fairly quickly, she should probably take us out of the running. She responded with, "Can you pick her up Wednesday?"

What?! I was dumbfounded. Shocked. Utterly baffled. What in mercy's name was God up to? The director gave us the night to pray and talk it over. The next morning, we were still perplexed. How do you pack your entire life to leave the country and have a new baby at the same time? What if the adoption stalls and one of us can't leave the country? Do we split our family up for weeks, possibly months? What if, what if, what if? It seemed so out of God's character to dangle carrots in front of our noses, so surely there wasn't a right or wrong answer... or was there?

I went to Tim with many tears and admitted that I was not capable of making this decision from an objective stand point. She had me at "baby girl" and my heart was all in. But I trusted him and would understand, even if I had to grieve for a time, whatever choice he made. I just really needed *him* to make it. Talk about a convenient moment to become the submissive wife! Tim went for a long walk and when he came back, his eyes were red and puffy. "I don't know how we're going to do this but I don't have to know," he said. "She's already mine in my heart. We're going to need some baby stuff!"

I asked the agency for one extra day to get things ready and then I skipped church that Wednesday night and headed to Walmart. I was like a maniac, flying through the baby department, almost literally chunking things into my cart: onesies, socks, bottles, pacifiers, hair bows, booties, blankets. If it was pink or ruffled, into the basket it went. That night, right before bed, we gathered the three kids up onto our bed and shared the news with them. And then Thursday afternoon, we came home with a twelve day old china doll - Isabella. Her name was very special to me. First because it was after my precious grandmother, Isabel Harrington. And secondly, because I was still able to honor my heroine (Sojourner Truth's given name was Isabella Baumfree) and by doing so, to harness a little bit of Journey's story into this new chapter.

Life was insane. There were boxes everywhere; there were boxes of stuff; there were piles of stuff that needed to be boxed; there were piles of stuff that needed to be sorted to be boxed; there was stuff that needed to be piled to be sorted to be boxed. You get the picture. Everything was evaluated by strict criteria: Is it necessary? Is it absolutely necessary? How much does it weigh? Anything that failed the test was sentenced to the yard sale pile. We had to sell whatever couldn't be transported or would be easier to purchase overseas. That included most of our furniture, the bulk of our winter clothes, and tons of décor items. Oh, and our house. We needed to sell our house. The market was horrible - this was the beginning of the Fannie Mae/Freddie Mac fiasco - but in the unlikely possibility that we sold the house before our departure date, we would need a place to live.

Friends from church graciously offered to let us live rent free in a newly refurbished apartment nestled atop a barn, overlooking a pasture full of cows. It was only one bedroom technically within a large open floor plan, but it was more than enough for as little time as we thought we would need it. Then, to the surprise of everyone, our house sold in ten days. Ten days. We sold what we could, stored what we couldn't, and moved to our temporary home. It was quaint. All six of us in about nine hundred square feet of living space. Mamoune's room was the walk-in closet. There was just enough space for her twin mattress and a box of clothes. The boys shared the empty laundry room (there was a second one down stairs with appliances hooked up). We had to line their beds up in an L-shape to make them both fit. And the baby Bella slept in a pack-n-play right there in the living room.

We needed a certain amount of money to get started, then a certain amount in commitments over the next year to "qualify" as missionaries. When we were nearly at our goal, Tim put in a call to the accountant to find out exactly where and how to deposit our funding. She had no idea who we were. *Had never even heard our names.* Mind you, this was a very small operation: the CEO, the director, and the accountant were the only official positions. Everything else was volunteer-based. Here we were, less than two months from our intended departure date, with thousands of dollars in our possession, and there was no account for us because the accountant did not even know we existed. It was a red flag we could not ignore. The weight of having so many people entrusting us with their money, in good faith believing that we would do the most and best with it, was immense. We were simply not willing to damage that trust or our testimony by continuing with this group. Another door…closed. We were very disappointed. Not long after our friends left that mission and went to work with a much more reputable ministry in Port-au-Prince, Haiti (www.heartlinehaiti.com), and continue to do amazing work there.

Now we were faced with a new dilemma. We were living in a barn with four kids and very few furnishings. Thankfully, Tim still had a job. Most importantly, we still had a desire to serve. Somewhere. Anywhere. So back to the Christian drawing board we went: prayer. Tim took a twist on the classic WWJD and began asking where would Jesus live? If he were to show up right here in good old central North Carolina, where would he be most likely to hang out? We searched the scripture and saw certain patterns in Jesus' relationships. He seemed to favor the poor over the rich, the sick over the well, the party crowd over the church crowd, and anybody that the world seemed to overlook, whether intentionally or not.

Thanks to the scouting eyes of a good friend, we discovered, purchased, and moved into a home in the low income area of town right across the street from government housing. The "projects," if you must. For a couple of years we juggled church ministry and neighborhood ministry. We combined the two whenever possible, taking groups of kids to church every week, but there was an inner conflict brewing and something new was on the horizon. But first came the something new that no one was expecting. It starts with a familiar line: we answered the phone.

The world's sweetest social worker was on the other end of the line. She asked in a timid voice, "Are you sitting down?" and then proceeded to inform me that Isabella was a big sister to a baby boy born just five days earlier. It was up to us, of course, but their birth mom was hoping we'd be willing to adopt him so they could be together. I could tell you that we prayed about it. We didn't. He was ours. Right then. That moment. No need for discussion.

We had six days to run around like absolute maniacs, filing paperwork, having medical exams, submitting fingerprints. The three oldest were immediately suspicious. I think it was Mamoune who finally said, "This feels like all the stuff we had to do when Bella showed up." Can't sneak another kid in past those guys. The next Tuesday, we welcomed home our ten day-old baby boy, Justus.

Over the next year, the battle between church life and missionary life continued to grow. Tim's focus as the Pastor of Evangelism was teaching others to "love your neighbor as yourself" and to share the gospel with whomever God placed in your sphere of influence. Our sphere was packed full but our availability was limited and we felt that God was asking us to *show* more than tell.

In 2009, after months of prayer and deliberation, we created a new ministry and filed for non-profit status. Tim left his church employment after ten years and we plunged in as full-time missionaries. It was terrifying. And liberating. And terrifying. Did I mention terrifying? There were lots of options when it came to the financial ordering of the new ministry. We researched and talked to friends who were doing the same type of ministry. In the end, we considered the example of a hero of the faith, George Mueller, and decided to keep our personal finances separate from the non-profit. We would do little to no marketing on our own behalf. Instead, we would make our needs known to God and trust Him to provide. We continued to connect ministry with our local church but had much more freedom to extend our services to the community. We did homework and tutoring in the afternoons, we helped with transportation to doctor's appointments during the day, and above all, just tried to love on people and build relationships.

One such relationship quickly developed into true and abiding friendship. Who would've thought that a couple of moms in their pajamas chatting at the bus stop would become like sisters? But we did. Melissa and I became proverbial peas in a pod. She was always our first volunteer, and with a huge family and no shortage of drama, she kept us on our toes. In one year's time, I was blessed to photograph a family wedding and to be in the room as two of Melissa's grandbabies made their grand entrance into the world. We were also there as her precious niece, having suffered a horrific act of brutality, left this world. We prayed together often, cried together often, and laughed our asses off on a regular basis. Occasionally, we fought but it was rare and never long-lived. Melissa was the kind of woman who loves with her whole heart. All in. And tells it like it was, no pulling punches. We were a lot alike and I can't imagine those years without her.

Documenting all the ups and downs, what we did right, what we did wrong, the best moments, the worst fights, the organizations that came and went, the churches who supported us because "it's good for *our* members" and then dropped us when the focus shifted from volunteer-driven work to just us loving and living out the gospel, the friends of ours who became true friends of our neighbors and continue to stick with us, the neighbors who became true friends…well, it would be a book within a book. Our departure from the church and the shifts in ministry over the next few years are detailed more in the second half of this book.

Another Note from the Author

My goal for this first section was simply to outline the ways that Christ was the center of our lives and the plum line by which we measured almost every decision from childhood, to dating, to marriage and children, to ministry. There was no "fake it 'til you make it." We were not "playing church." We were not "working our way into heaven." These are the claims that have been made and will no doubt continue. But let me remind you that if you didn't know that we left the faith, this entire account would simply be my testimony and few would question it. Neither my salvation nor my motives would be challenged. It would be accepted exactly as it is, as it should be.

Unlike the first, the second half is this book isn't necessarily chronological. Certain sections are simply meant to expand on how I reached new conclusions related to some of the issues in our family and in today's culture. Also, please understand that I realize there are many, many different types of Christians and churches in the world. There are liberal, liturgical, progressive, gay, emergent, catholic, cultural, charismatic, independent, pacifists, militants, etc. And I know that not all of these groups of people share views, convictions, and interpretations on all matters of Christian life. I not only know this but talk quite at length about it in an upcoming section. For this reason, I feel it is necessary to explain that when I make statements regarding the general thoughts or beliefs of "Christians" and "churches" I am referring to those most prevalent in both my experience and my geography – those who lean heavily toward conservatism, Biblical inerrancy, and a literalistic interpretation of scripture.

Part Three: On Shaky Ground

Kawasaki Baby

> "Faith does not give you the answers, it just stops you asking the questions."
> -Frater Ravus

It was November 2010. My youngest son, Justus, was two years old. It was flu season and it seemed everyone we knew had some form of "the crud" running through their families. So it wasn't a big surprise when Justus began running a fever. We gave him Tylenol to rest at night and plenty of snuggle time on the couch during the day. It was a weekend and we decided to watch him until Monday and then take him to the doctor if he was no better or had worsened. On Sunday he broke out in a rash on his back and stomach. I searched the internet for a possible cause and learned that the strep bacteria can sometimes lead to Scarlet Fever. I called the doctor first thing Monday morning.

By the time of his appointment, the rash had spread to his legs and upper arms. A rapid strep test confirmed (in error) what the doctor suspected. They gave him a shot of antibiotics and the expectation that he would be feeling much better within twenty-four hours. By Tuesday night his fever had spiked to 105.8. The doctor switched him to a broad-spectrum antibiotic and we waited to see improvement. And waited. Despite giving him alternating doses of acetaminophen and ibuprofen around the clock, his temperature never dropped below 103 degrees.

I'd been sleeping on the couch with him for almost a week and was nearing complete exhaustion. He writhed and wriggled constantly and didn't want to be anywhere but in my arms. His fever was so high at times it actually felt like my own skin was burning against him. At best, I dozed sitting up, soaked with my own sweat while trying to keep him comfortable. Mostly, I prayed. I cried and I prayed. I begged God to break the fever. I begged Him to let the medicine work. I begged him to heal my little boy. I reminded Him of His promises and that He was the one who brought this little fellow into our lives. I pleaded for Him to show up.

After another trip to the doctor's office, more blood work and still no answers, we were told that if he did not show improvement or any other symptoms appeared by the next morning, we should take him to the emergency room. Morning came, and not only was there no relief, his hands and feet were swollen twice their normal size and he was now reluctant to move, complaining of pain in the back of his neck. I feared meningitis. We headed to the ER.

Our anxiety only grew as one doctor after another after another came and went. Finally they reached a consensus and attempted to inform us, "We believe your son has Kawasaki Syndrome." Tim and I stared blankly. This condition was so foreign to us we didn't even know what questions to ask. I remember them using the words "medical phenomenon" and thinking *that cannot be good.* "The problem is" they continued explaining, "There is no test for this syndrome. Basically, we will start treatment and a favorable reaction will confirm the diagnosis." It felt a little hit or miss but it was all we had to go on, so for the third time that week, we held our baby boy down on a table as blood was drawn and IV's were set.

By the next evening his fever was gone and his fingers and toes, though peeling in thick layers of dead skin, were almost back to their usual size. The treatment was working and as long as his temperature stayed down he would be released the following afternoon. This news brought great relief, but that second night in the hospital, my mind was restless.

The nurse came in around three in the morning to check his vitals and give him another dose of baby aspirin. Justus thought it was candy and was an extremely compliant little patient in that regard. After getting him snuggled back under the white sheets and sneaking my purse from near the pull-out bed where Tim was sleeping, I camped out in the restroom for some much needed processing.

I cried. At first, I cried for all that could still go wrong: a relapse, long-term heart damage. I cried for all that had gone right: the treatment was working and we were not still wondering what was wrong with him. I cried out all of the fear I'd been hiding for days; I cried out all the relief I was feeling as his body recuperated. Then, I cried for what I felt most of all – complete abandonment. I had no idea where God was through all of this. I took a scrap of paper from my purse and began writing just as the thoughts came to me:

Where is the Power?

If I'm honest with myself; if I stand here bare-boned in
naked truth
I find that I'm asking where's the proof?
The apparent evidence lacking
has me back-tracking
to a place where doubts and skepticism take root.

What are the contradictions;
the implications?
Is it that or
is it simply a matter
 of time, will, sovereignty
and other dimensions my eyes can't see?

If I ask You to heal now and You don't
or You won't
are You less faithful for Your hesitation?
Or do I judge you *more* faithful having endured the
situation?
Dare I judge you at all?
Judge not, lest judgment fall.

But what of this faith that moves mountains
or drives fountains up from rolling seas
letting thousands cross on sandy ground;
while I drown in my own sea of sand sinking quick?
Do tests of faith strengthen hope
or does hope deferred make the heart sick?

When Jesus prayed in dismay, "Let this cup pass from me"
was His obedience too great,
or was His faith just too weak?
If I ask will *I* receive?

How can I believe, if I must submit
all the while admit that He answers as He pleases?
Or has He deceived us?

"Heresy!" cries the Pharisee.
You whose eyebrows are raised in disgrace;
scowling face.
"How could she?"
"Why would she say such a thing,
absurd, profane.
As though God is obligated to explain."

But these questions in my mind
long to be satisfied
and this temptation to deny
shouldn't surprise
or compromise
the love He bestows
if He already knows
what anxiety lies inside of me;
striving to walk the Gospel in the midst of *this* reality:

That pain remains the same
and the rain is unchanged
falling on the just and the unjust
but must I be crazy
to think that maybe
I could access special favor
Having put my trust in this Savior?

If a father knows how to give good gifts to his own
And when his child asks for bread wouldn't hand him a stone
How much more does our Father in heaven,
the Father of Lights, know how to give us good…

Wait.
How does God define good?

Good is good, right?
A word with a definition
a meaning that creates expectation,
anticipation of something…
well…good.

But is a child dying,
parents crying, trying
to understand
what's coming from His hand good?

A million people in an earthquake
that shakes, and breaks,
and devastates
their lives already in a precarious state;
is *that* good?

Cars crash, thieves dash
down dark alleyways
to easy escapes;
Innocent falling prey
to scams and schemes
Wall Street exploiting dreams
with its greed
A child's soul bleeds under the invasion
of a pedophiles' touch
it's all too much!

And since sooner or later we will all die
Why shouldn't I cry
"God, is *this* good?!"

It was the first time ever I allowed myself to ask the questions without feeling obligated to give the "right" answers. I knew all the clichés, all the Sunday school responses, and all the hermeneutical juggling of the seminary crowd. I knew all about "in His time" and "mysterious ways" and "without God the doctors couldn't have helped." But deep in my heart I cried, "Bullshit! Where were you?" I still believed in God and the faith tradition I'd always known but suddenly sovereignty was huge source of confusion and frustration. Let me explain further.

I hate traffic. I specifically hate having to cross traffic. When I first got my driver's license, I would drive two blocks out of the way making all right hand turns to get to my favorite fast food joint. And as an adult, I continued to face multi-lane left hand turns with dread. Each time I would pray for a "clear shot" across the sea of cars, not just some rote muttering but a sincere prayer believing that God cared about the little things in my life. Once I was safely across, I set the example for my kids by thanking Jesus for loving us so much.

I distinctly remember the day I stood in the bathroom with angry tears stinging the backs of my eyes and asked Tim, "Why do I believe that Jesus gives a shit about me crossing the highway if he doesn't care that my kid is dying?" Again, I wasn't yet questioning God's existence, only His method of interaction with us, or at least the Christian (myself included) representation of Him. It made God appear trite and trivial to hear one person praising him for helping them find their car keys while another prayed for the safe return of their missing child only to find his mutilated body in a desolate field, miles from home. Doesn't it seem reasonable that the God who says "children are a heritage from the Lord" would care more about the twenty-six thousand of them who will die of starvation than he does whether or not it rains on your church's yard sale day? One wouldn't think so after reading a single day's worth of typical Christian Facebook statuses.

This sort of "genie in a bottle" God shows up time and time again. Many (thankfully even some Christians) called into question the continuous stream of accolades given God by 2012 Olympic Gold medalist Gabrielle Douglas. Quotes from interviews, tweets, Facebook, and even the comments of teammates would have us all believing that is was simply God's will for this young lady to win gold. The problem arises when we deduce the logical inverse of this hypothesis: it was God's will to devastate the dreams and aspirations of a young Russian girl. No one really wants to say this because it doesn't sound much like the loving God we all applaud and yet that's exactly what's being implied. If God determined the winner, God determined the loser. Sorry Victoria Komova – while you may have been just as talented and certainly worked as hard and sacrificed as much, you just weren't prayed up like our girl Gabby.

Likewise, Ray Lewis, linebacker for the Baltimore Ravens, winners of the 2013 Superbowl, quoted scripture after clinching the AFC championship. "No weapon formed against me will prosper. No weapon. No weapon," he repeated passionately before the cameras. While I personally don't know many Bible scholars who would entertain the notion that the prophet Isaiah was referring to football, Mr. Lewis put it out there just the same. Never mind the pesky reality of Christian players on the opposing team or Christian fans cheering for the opposing team. They all fell short of the mark while Lewis and his teammates clearly provoked the favor of the great God Almighty in order to secure that coveted graven image, er, I mean, trophy.

I know I'm being a bit of a smartass here. I admit it. But the condescending tone I use in these examples is the same one I was using to examine my own experiences. How arrogant could I be to credit an omnipotent deity for a good parking spot at the mall while entire countries were ravaged by war, poverty, and disease with little divine (or human for that matter) intervention? Did I really believe it was the "grace of God" that I'd been born in the United States as I'd heard countless times in my life? How? How could I without realizing that this belief is laden with the accusation that God is withholding grace from lesser nations? Could God really be that stingy or were we really that stupid?

As I said before, the questions that surfaced during Justus' illness were not the proverbial "straw that broke the camel's back," but they would prove to be the first snagged thread in the unraveling tapestry of my faith. It was uncomfortably clear to me as we were discharged that Sunday from the Wake Med Children's Hospital at the very moment the Hindu family of the child two doors down was being called in to say their goodbyes that it couldn't possibly all come down to grace, or favor, or answered prayer. I had no more right to leave with a healthy child than they did and there was nothing they had done to deserve such heartbreak. It felt more like dumb luck than anything else.

A new awareness was stirred. I listened to Christians differently from that day. I *heard* their words differently from that day. I saw the flip side – the inherent reciprocal of God's failure to act on behalf of some amid the boasts of His providence by others. And for all that I didn't know, I now knew, at least, that I knew less than I'd known before.

RAD... Really RAD

> "There are wounds that never show on the body that are deeper and more hurtful than anything that bleeds."
>
> **Laurell K. Hamilton, *Mistral's Kiss***

The next year passed as had the years before it. That's not to say it was uneventful. "Uneventful" had vanished from our vocabulary on the same day our oldest daughter appeared. Mamoune had just turned three when we met her and was almost five when we finally brought her home from her birthplace of Haiti.

We had already adopted our two sons, Nathan and Isaiah, when we traveled to Port-au-Prince for a nine day mission trip. It may sound naïve given that we worked, ate, and slept in an orphanage, but we had no intentions of adopting again at that time. We were looking to love on "the least of these" while challenging our cultural awareness and frankly, orphanages in Haiti are like gas stations here – one on every corner. It was a good six weeks post trip when adopting Mamoune became a thought, another two weeks to see it as a possibility, and two years to become a done deal.

Ironically, on September 11, 2003 we picked up our very own international terrorist. I know it's hard to imagine an underweight, malnourished four year old wreaking havoc on two more-or-less rational adults but I assure you, she took over our home and held it hostage for almost eight years. To give the detailed account of those years would mean to finish another book in and of itself, including (but not limited to) thousands of battles, voodoo trances, slammed doors, broken furniture, suicide threats, murder threats, sleeping with one eye open, injuries to siblings, too many spankings, too many tears, and too little understanding.

We had never heard the words "Reactive Attachment Disorder" and to be fair, probably wouldn't have listened if we'd been warned. Our worldview didn't favor behavioral labels or mental health diagnoses. We addressed discipline in much simpler terms of sin or submission. Anything else was psychobabble meant to distract from the root problem of all humanity: depravity.

Of course, now we see that Mamoune was never alone in her siege. She had hundreds of unwitting accomplices: a church full. None accurately imagining the hell we lived behind closed doors and none realizing that there best efforts to encourage us with biblical principles only served to bury us deeper in conflict with ourselves and our child. The times we reached out to friends, family, pastors, Christian counselors (both lay and professional), we were given a standard line. "She's just a normal little sinner and with good biblical parenting and lots of prayer, Jesus can fix it." In truth, the individual conversations were more varied but the take away was pretty much always the same and always that simplistic. And so, we continued year after excruciating year and I waffled constantly between guilt – *I need to control my temper, I need to pray harder, I need to parent more consistently* - and condemnation – *She* needs to control herself, *she* needs to pray more, *she* needs to obey. Between the two of us there was always someone to blame.

Occasionally, I searched outside sources for something, anything that might bring relief. I read books from secular authors who seemed to know just what I was going through, the check list of possible symptoms was enough to make my heart scream, "This is my child! She's not a 'normal' kid. She needs help! I need help!" But I could not commit myself to their methods because they said nothing of sin and selfishness and were only offering temporary bandages for an eternal disease. Meanwhile, the help that came from "acceptable" sources was proving to be no help at all.

In September of 2011, almost eight years to the day of her homecoming, we reached an all-time low. Mamoune's rage episodes had grown stronger and more physically violent, just as she was growing stronger. They were also more frequent as pre-teen hormones surged. My own health was deteriorating from the stress and the adrenaline that came with each new eruption. I was having panic attacks, heart palpitations, grinding my teeth in fitful sleep, and those were just the physical manifestations. Emotionally I was a wreck. We were always either in the middle of a showdown or on pins and needles waiting for the next episode. Every member of the family felt it. Mamoune's screaming fits terrified the two youngest. Her efforts to sabotage holidays and family outings left the older boys feeling angry and neglected. And I felt like I was failing all of them in a million ways. We were ready to end it, to do the one thing we'd swore would never happen to us. I was googling stories of adoption disruption and looking for an out.

One particular afternoon, I left the house in tears. I had to get out and breathe and think. I drove to a nearby park intending to stroll along the path and let the fresh air and scenery calm my nerves, but as soon as my feet hit the pavement, I was off. I couldn't have slowed down if I'd wanted to. My body was determined to pound all of that pent-up emotion into the concrete and not only were my legs on autopilot but my thoughts were pouring out unchecked, uncensored. I don't recall seeing another person on the track that day and it's a good thing since I'm certain I looked and sounded like a complete lunatic.

I held nothing back. I was done. I couldn't handle anymore – the fights, the tears, the constant cloud of hatred emanating from my child's eyes no matter what I did or didn't do, the vigilance required to keep the other children safe from her outbursts, the exhaustion of criticism from family members who knew nothing of our reality and yet seemed to have all the answers. It was over and I needed God to know it. I had begged Him to change her heart and things were worse than ever. I wanted her to stop playing the "poor adopted me" card and start taking responsibility. I wanted to stop putting her birth mom on a pedestal for "doing the hard thing" as though my end of the deal was easy as pie. I needed God to either do something or let me off the fucking hook, and that's exactly what I told Him.

I finally slowed down and lay on a park bench staring up into the branches of the trees. My mind wandered through all the years, all the books, the articles, the web searches, the counseling appointments. Then I came to the one thing I'd been intentionally pushing out of my thoughts – a friend of a friends' website. This woman had RAD kids. She had several. She wore her hair in dreads and donned obnoxiously colorful knee socks. She said things like "out-crazy the crazy" and "our kids don't need to be fixed; they need to be loved" and frankly, I hated her. She was doing all the things my gut knew I needed to be doing and was she doing them unapologetically. She seemed to assume her kids were amazing and just needed help to realize it and accept it. She didn't assume that they were innately sinful and needed to be made aware of their brokenness before a perfect God. She talked about trauma and abandonment as though they were legitimate wounds, not just excuses for acting out. She shared honest anger towards her kid's actions but literally dripped with compassion for them at the exact same time. I soaked it up when she talked about parents like us needing help and date nights and respite, but I balked at her tactics because I couldn't shave them down or reconfigure them enough to beat them into the square hole of "biblical parenting" I *knew* was right.

That's when I heard it. A voice speaking right into my ear saying, "You want all of the sympathy and none of the responsibility. You are no different from your daughter." In other words, stop complaining about the diagnosis if you're not willing to invest in the treatment. I thought it was God. It had to be God because I sure as hell wouldn't have pointed the finger back at myself. I was looking for a way out and this, this voice, was pointing in, *way* in, deeper than I wanted to go. It was so counter intuitive and for a while I believed it was God. I told people it was God. And maybe in some universal way that transcends the Yahweh box, it was. But looking back even just a few weeks later, I suspected the truth. It was me. My voice. The same voice I'd heard and ignored for years. It was the voice I had tentatively shared and intuitively swallowed in the presence of Christian friends. So why pass it off as "thus sayeth the Lord"? It's because subconsciously I knew my options were limited. Thus sayeth Amie's instincts? Years of experience? Inner wisdom? Liberal blogger chick? No chance in hell any of those would make the cut, so my brain formatted it in a context that would allow me to pursue the help we needed while maintaining the approval of our sphere.

I headed home from the park that day and shared my "revelation" with Tim. We agreed that it was time to search out a therapist who specialized in adoption regardless of his or her religious affiliation. It was time for us to let Mamoune's past inform our interaction with her instead of relying on an ancient text, all the while dismissing the history she herself had lived through.

There were no such therapists in our immediate area, so based on reviews and longevity of practice, we chose one that was located about an hour from our home. We didn't tell Mamoune where we were going until we had almost reached our destination. We knew she would be less than thrilled and wanted to avoid having to wrestle her into the van. Once we explained the nature of our outing, she was mad. *Really mad.* Fortunately, *really mad* was no more or less mad than usual for her. We spent the last few minutes of the drive emphasizing the need for her to be as honest as possible about everything; even things that may be embarrassing to her or to us. Goodness knows there were enough mistakes to go around. More than anything, we wanted her to know that this was about us and not just her. It was *our* therapy and we all had plenty of work to do. I wrote the following excerpt shortly after that first appointment.

"Bedraggled. Yes. That is how we must have appeared. Despite our best attempts to seem well put together, we no doubt arrived at the therapist's office looking exactly as we were. Wounded. Stressed. Tired. Bedraggled.

The therapist spoke to us as though we were clear-thinking, mentally competent adults. That was nice of her but I knew she could see it. Even without her training, there was no missing the neon sign hanging over our heads flashing "damaged goods" in steady rhythm.

We truly were damaged goods. Having been dismissed by peers and pastors with misguided sympathies and simplistic answers laden with guilt and condemnation, having had our struggle denied and then twisted into accusations of abuse by our parents, and most of all having been rejected and scorned by our own daughter in ways we never anticipated and could hardly understand, we were drowning in a sea of loneliness and helplessness.

But now, here we sat across from this woman with empathy in her eyes, who seemed to recognize our story even as it tumbled out of our mouths in a desperate, chaotic fashion. Here was bedraggled, wounded, stressed, tired, damaged us finding solace in acknowledgment.

Yes. That first day of therapy was like gasping in a deep breath after being held under water for a very. long. time."

Many, many sessions later, are we better off? Well, the answer is yes! We have all learned to put into practice the compassion, self-awareness, and space needed to heal. This has been easier for Mamoune since we incorporated birth control to balance her hormone levels and a low dose anti-depressant - two forms of "medicating" I swore I would NEVER do as a young Christian parent speaking out of the depths of ignorance. With this help, she is able to receive the therapy prompts before the trauma swallows her up, processing her feelings more openly and being willing to accept help to climb out of those dark places. This is huge. We are learning to trust each other and to be okay if our mother/daughter relationship doesn't look like the perfect ideal we'd been pressuring ourselves with for so long.

As for Tim and me, the therapist gave us three things that I believe changed our lives. The first, as mentioned in the above excerpt, was simple validation. We were not alone. The second thing therapy gave us was the ability to see our child through the eyes of scientific observation and not spiritual oppression. Mamoune's behaviors were not the result of a deviant heart rebelling against God. In fact, most of them were rooted in shame and self-loathing and the last thing she needed to hear was that the God of the universe (the same one who allowed for the trauma and abuse she'd suffered) was disappointed in her ability to cope. How fucked up is that?

In reality, Mamoune has physiological triggers and responses that are as difficult for her to control as it would be for you to avoid blinking when someone claps inches from your face. And while I admit that I still get frustrated and wish that progress came faster, shifting focus from "spiritual heart issue" to scientific brain function spelled emotional freedom for both of us.

The third gift our therapist gave us was a virtual toolbox full of new ways to respond, new ways to listen, new ways to protect all of our children, to stop martyring ourselves, to take time when we need it, to acknowledge and accept our own emotional triggers and limits, and to give everyone in our house space to process this unusual thing we call a family without fear of eternal consequences and abandonment.

What of that dread-lock-crazy-sock-liberal-hippie-blogger-chic I mentioned earlier? She's a great friend and I owe her a perpetual debt of gratitude for prompting the "true" voice of reason in my head that September day. And she's a top-notch parenting coach with a kick-ass blog that you can check out for yourself: www.welcometomybrain.net or on Facebook under "Christine Moers – Therapeutic Parenting Coach."

Not unlike Justus' illness, Mamoune presented us with yet another situation in which science, medicine, and psychology offered tangible, measurable results after faith failed to yield anything but more trauma and more questions.

The Business of Church

> "Man is kind enough when not excited by religion."
>
> -Mark Twain, *A Horse's Tale*

I met my husband when I was sixteen and he was seventeen. Aside from the year he spent at a liberal arts school in Indiana and our recent two-year stint under non-profit status, he has been employed in church ministry all of our twenty-three years together. The specific roles have changed over the years: janitor, choir director, youth pastor, pastor of outreach, and so on. Behind each of those positions lie stories of people we loved and who loved us, showing us incredible hospitality and support. Then there are those who presented immense challenges.

Now, I know full well that airing out a list of grievances against the church and various members can be cast off as petty. If this were merely a gripe session allowing me to "get some things off my chest," I would wholeheartedly agree. Bitching for bitching's sake may feel good on occasion but does tend to burn more bridges than it builds. At the risk of striking that match, I cannot figure out how to tell my story without including some of these experiences. It's not about the specific people or even the specific hurt inflicted. It's about the measure of each incident and the culmination of all of them as catalysts moving us through the phases of this journey. These were not simple personality conflicts, nor were they contributors to our divergence from the faith at the time they occurred. Quite the opposite. Each one pushed us deeper into the Word, deeper into our desire to know, understand, and defend scripture, and deeper into our conviction to follow Jesus.

The church Tim and I belonged to as a young couple suffered a split about a year before we were married. I'd love to say that this is an unusual event in the life of the church, but unless you've been living under a rock your entire life, you know better. Half the congregation stayed. Half left. We were among the latter. The small group of dissenters met in homes for a time. We were one of "those" churches. Eventually, property was purchased and we began formulating outreach programs for the surrounding community. Among these, a fall festival organized by yours truly.

We printed colorful flyers and blanketed every parking lot within a five mile radius. There was a large mobile home park not far from our location so we divided into two person teams and walked every street making personal invitations to the residents. At one house, my partner and I were greeted by two young girls who willingly drug their mom to the door to talk to us about the "party." Their mom took the flyer but shook her head. "I don't have a car," she explained. Two long faces looked up at us. "Well, I could pick them up," I offered.

She eyed me, half surprised, half suspicious. "You'd do that?" she asked incredulously. I assured her it was no trouble. The festival was scheduled to begin at nine in the morning the following Saturday so we made arrangements to pick the girls up at about ten 'til.

The church members, aka "set up crew," were asked to arrive at seven-thirty that bitterly cold October morning. At seven-thirty, there were three people present including myself and Tim. It was eight-thirty and later as the rest began trickling in. Granted, one family's pipes had frozen overnight (I mentioned bitterly cold), a perfectly reasonable explanation for being so late. In fact, I'm sure that everyone had perfectly reasonable explanations but there was so much to do and no possible way to be done in time. Knowing why did little to curb my disappointment and I told them as much. I was quickly chastised for having unrealistic expectations of my volunteers. Unfortunately, it wasn't *my* expectations nagging at the back of my thoughts. It was the expectation of two little girls who would be anxiously waiting for me and the reputation of Christ that I had put on the line. I felt trapped between two ideologies: to be like Paul who seemed to emphasize ministry to the brethren; or to be like Jesus who seemed to favor the outcast.

When we were finally ready and I was able to slip away, it was after ten o'clock, more than an hour past the pickup time we'd agreed on. I was greeted at the door by squeals and hugs. Again, mom eyed me from her spot on the couch. "I told 'em you weren't coming," she said flatly. I swallowed the lump that leapt into my throat and apologized profusely. She still agreed to let the girls come with me and they had a great time, racking up on candy and prizes. I decided that day that I would always err on the side of the stranger, the foreigner, the leper, the prostitute, the fatherless, the least of these.

That church eventually dissolved for many reasons and a short time later we found ourselves at a small church in central Georgia. Tim accepted the position of Music & Youth Pastor, a horrible combination that has spelled burnout for many young ministers, as either one is a full-time job in and of itself.

We bought a starter home in neighboring Milledgeville, which was a bit of a joke in my family. I knew one thing about the town prior to moving there: it had once been home to the state's infamous asylum. I remember my parents teasingly threatening to pack my Grandmother's bags and ship her to Milledgeville when she would have "spells." Now here we were taking residence voluntarily. My dad would say, "Well, we always knew somebody in this family would end up there."

The church was a stone's throw from Lake Sinclair, which made for some really beautiful sunrise services…and an underlying competition between lake life and church life. Even so, things progressed well for several years. The choir grew steadily and thrived under Tim's direction. The youth group grew rapidly and constantly kept us on our toes. The music showcased Tim's natural talent, but those kids were our heart, and in some way, our undoing. We pushed them hard and sometimes they pushed back. There was always the tricky attempt to balance friendship with authority and fielding the dynamic between parents and teens. But for as much as we fought with them, we fought for them. There were those in the church who saw the youth as a by-product of good, tithing families but not so much a worthy focus. We couldn't have disagreed more and so, conflict ensued: relationships and relevant outreach versus buildings and tradition. It all came to a head one fateful night.

It was a Wednesday night service on April 20, 1999. Just twenty-four hours after the shootings at Columbine High School and the town of Littleton, Colorado was forced into the national spotlight. That event (and the unfortunate many that have followed, right up to the 2012 Sandy Hook massacre) was by no means isolated in its impact. We all felt it. And our youth, almost two thousand miles away also felt it. As they filed into the basement youth room that night, the energy was different. The usual cut-ups were not cutting up, the usual trouble-makers were subdued, and from an age group that typically masks its feeling with obnoxious behavior, there was a rare vulnerability in their openness. There worlds had been rattled and they wanted, needed to feel grounded and connected. Our praise band assembled and we began our worship set with a remarkably captive audience.

This is where the trouble started. Church growth always brings with it the question of buildings and with that, the question of finances. For some ungodly reason which could never be determined, the powers that be scheduled a meeting of the finance committee that very night, not in one of the fifteen empty classrooms across the way, but in the room directly situated above our youth room and subsequently, our sound system.

We were three chords into our first song when a representative deacon made his way down the stairs. "We're having a meeting upstairs. Could you wait about ten or fifteen minutes?" Well, okay. That was easy enough. We took some prayer request and debriefed about the recent shootings. Fifteen minutes later, our drummer counted us off. We made it a few bars this time before deacon number two appeared and requested another short delay. *Oh-kay*. Tim went ahead with his planned devotion. More talking. More praying. Twenty minutes passed and we were well beyond the half-way point in our service when we figured surely it was safe to proceed.

One verse in, there was a loud pop followed by dead silence as the amps went out as well as half the lights in the room. Fearing we'd accidentally blown a fuse, Tim headed up to investigate, where he was promptly met by the visibly irate deacon who'd thrown the breaker to shut us down once and for all. When Tim returned to explain the situation, the rest of us were dumbfounded, followed quickly by royally pissed. My calm and controlled husband talked the rest of us off the ledge and suggested we close the night out praying. Of course, by this point we were running over our time but we were all in need of some closure to this emotionally charged night, so the kids circled up to pray. And that is what we were doing when the pastor himself shuffled down the stairs and announced, "Tim, you need to get upstairs. You have a choir loft full of adults waiting for you." I stared in disbelief. Tim conceded with reserved agitation and headed to his next post. I didn't bother attending choir practice that night. I paced the building and grounds alternating between crying, fuming, and most likely, cursing.

I couldn't believe the irony. Teenagers had heartlessly murdered their classmates and then taken their own lives but our church leaders were aggressively combating the desire of our own teenagers to worship. It was another case of the business of the church taking precedence over the business of the Father. Retelling it even now leaves me shaking my head.

Things deteriorated quickly. There was an incident involving two of our boys and an altercation with their step-father that had turned physical. A meeting was arranged for the parents, several deacons, the pastor, and Tim and me. Earlier in the book, I regarded myself as tender-hearted and compassionate. These things are true of me but should never be mistaken for soft-spoken or cowardly. In line with my natural red hair, the emphasis in compassion is on *passion*. I sat patiently listening as the men of the group discussed the situation. There were many suggestions for implementing safeguards, references to parenting strategies, and subtle inferences to church discipline. They were all saying the right things but there was something in the tone that felt more like political side-stepping than actual intervention. Not having lived my whole life in this town, perhaps I didn't feel the same obligation of relationship to this man that others must have. Figuring I had nothing to lose, I interjected my perspective just before the meeting was adjourned. "If you lay a hand on any of these kids again, I will call DSS myself."

It was not an empty threat, but it was one I never had to act on. Someone else beat me to it. Of course, this gentleman believed (and probably still does to this day) that I made the call. I knew nothing of it or the visit he received from social services until those he'd accused me to (pretty much the whole church) began questioning me. My denial was disregarded but frankly, I could not have cared less what this man thought of me and would certainly have thanked whoever reported him. Needless to say, that relationship remained strained.

There were other red flags over the years, and it's safe to say the camel was already limping hard on the night the "last straw" was thrown. Discipleship classes were held for all church members during the hour before Sunday night services. They were poorly attended by the youth, who were not easily persuaded to leave the warm waters of the lake when there was still two hours of sunlight left to enjoy. We had divided the guys and girls into separate groups, and as luck would have it, I ended up with no one to teach that particular night. After waiting around for possible latecomers, and not wanting to disturb any classes already in progress, I slipped up the stairs and settled on the top step to eaves drop on the "Master Life" class being taught by the Pastor. I thought I'd catch a few minutes of in-depth teaching, my Bible open in my lap to follow along.

Instead of references to Matthew, however, I heard my own name and Tim's. Much of the proceeding conversation is a blur as I was trying to wrap my brain around what was happening. There were accusations. "They don't respect the Lord's house." Oh boy. That was the familiar voice of the man who'd thrown the breaker on us. The same man who berated the kids every time they dared dribble a ball on the sacred linoleum of the fellowship/dining hall.

"They love those kids and I don't think they're being treated fairly at all." Sigh. A defender. *Thank you.* Then came the pastor's summary. "They're immature and they just haven't been in the ministry long enough to understand how it works. They'll learn." If he meant putting the institution before the people, pussyfooting around confrontations, and being satisfied with a mediocre Christian life, those were lessons I never hoped to learn. In too many ways, the future (now the past) would work to prove him right. Within two weeks, Tim had tendered his resignation.

As I said before, I know that some readers will be convinced that I am just harping on petty insults and that surely all these little things add up to be contributors to our current cynicism ,but trust me when I say that there were plenty of reasons to bail from this particular church long before we did. For example, the Christmas sermon in which the pastor took great care explaining the importance of the prophet Simeon to the religious system of the day, followed by the prophetess Anna being likened to a janitor. According to him, she was probably responsible for keeping the candles lit and sweeping up the temple stairs. Let's recap: prophet = religious sage; prophetess = custodian. Throw in a dozen more sexist/racist remarks and you'll see that we stayed well beyond our tolerance level for the sake of the youth who we loved so much.

And far from questioning God at this time, we soon moved to Wake Forest, North Carolina where Tim would attend and eventually graduate from seminary. Still believing that greater understanding of Scripture and greater obedience to Scripture were key in this Christian life, we pressed in harder and dug in deeper.

In North Carolina, we got settled into our new apartment and soon settled into a new church. It was Baptist in name and doctrine but more Church of God in its contemporary worship. The preaching wasn't as exegetical as we'd hoped for but the people were sincere and loving and it was growing like crazy. It was a very exciting time and we jumped in with both feet. Soon, Tim began singing with the worship team and I followed shortly thereafter. About a year later, Tim was hired as a part-time music intern and choir director. Our choir kicked ass! I know, that's not appropriate to the context but it was true. They sang their guts out, they prayed their hearts out, and even at times when Tim challenged their style preferences, they trusted the leadership and poured themselves into every project. These were good times.

Unfortunately, all that glitters is not gold. Yeah, it's a cliché, but one that holds much truth.

The closer you get to the inner workings of a church the more you realize that it's as much business as the liquor store down the street. Past the shiny veneer, the stained glass windows, the free coffee, the sparkling chandeliers, what have you, it's a numbers game. People represent tithes which represent bigger buildings which represent more people which represent more tithes and on and on and on.

There is one church that I know of personally, who though not immune (because I think it's impossible to avoid), seems to have a more organic view of themselves and their parishioners. The Church Under the Bridge in Waco, Texas no doubt has its flaws but "business as usual" doesn't seem to be the obvious one. And since we have never been part of the administration of this particular church, you could accuse me of contradicting my own argument since my perspective is from outside the walls of the church, so to speak. But in my defense, it's fairly easy to do because there are no walls. Literally.

Sunday mornings under the speeding cars and rattling semi's traversing the bridge at I-35 and 4th Street, you will find a group of diverse worshippers gathered: black, white, Latino, old, young, doctors, students, addicts, tourists, homeless. In our short time visiting the church and the pastor and his wife, Jimmy and Janet Dorrell, I never got the sense that his overarching goal is to grow so large that they halt the traffic zooming above or to raise so much money that they can finally build a grand cathedral and get out of the blasted heat (or cold –it was absolutely freezing the day we attended). It seems that the primary goal is to love God and love one another. And regardless of how I feel about the former, I believe the latter is a universal principle and I have great respect for this ministry.

In our own church, there were lots of little things that snowballed into bigger things that eventually lead to our departure. Bothersome little things, like when reports from overseas mission teams were trumped at the last minute by special guest singers or when really huge world events went almost unmentioned in light of the order of service. One incident which really riled me up was in December as the church aired a video released by the International Mission Board to promote the Lottie Moon offering for international missions. We were by no means the only church showing the video, but I can't help but think that during the previewing of it, when they likened making a donation to the actual demise of this incredible missionary, somebody should've said, "Hold up!"

Seriously. The line was something like, "You, too, can participate in the suffering of Lottie Moon by making your donation..." This while a picture of Lottie Moon overlapped the image of someone scribbling out a check. What? The woman *starved* to death! War and famines and rampant disease in China had devastated the lives of the people she loved so much and she literally gave them the food from her own table to the point of starvation. "But you, too, can participate in her suffering by simply writing a check. And if you get a cramp in your hand from adding all those zeroes to your dollar amount, you're practically a martyr for Christ yourself" (wink-wink). Okay, they didn't say that. That's just me being a smartass. Again. But they really did make her death out to be a trite and trivial matter and that pissed me off.

It was hard to see a church where we once willingly sat on the gymnasium floor to make room for guests now choosing to spend an extra five to ten dollars per chair to get double-bun cushioning. Meanwhile, the poorest among us were viewed as a "wonderful" service project for our people, but otherwise an inconvenience. People became measured by their membership potential, not their humanity, and whether or not a ministry provided the best "Velcro factor" (how many people "stick") became more important than whether or not it reflected Christ.

Perhaps the greatest rub was the pastor's increasing political rants. Every week there seemed to be something – gun control, the slippery slope to Marxism, (if Obama won the election, that is - never stated in plain terms but always implied), the evils of evolution, etc. It became harder and harder to overlook. especially after we moved into the lowest income area of Wake Forest with the hopes of building relationships and doing full-time ministry.

Then came the clincher.

I don't remember what Scripture he was teaching (didn't usually matter anyway) or the three points of the sermon that were outlined in the bulletin. He lost me completely after saying, "People who live in government housing and want all these entitlements are justifying their laziness."

Even as I type it I have to stop and just stare out the window for a moment while my blood pressure regulates itself. My eyes widened like saucers and then the tears came. I couldn't believe what I was hearing for three reasons:

    1- Tim and I were sitting in line next to about ten or so children, all of whom lived in the projects. I hoped for once they were passing notes and not paying

attention lest they go home and repeat this to their parents.
2- There was no legitimate reason ever for a statement like this to be included in a sermon supposedly grounded in scripture. Even if he believed it, this was not the platform for sharing it.
3- Because I knew it wasn't fucking true! I knew the woman who got up and went to work at five-thirty every morning so she could be home with her kids after school in the afternoons. Hell, her kids were sitting right beside me. I knew that an increase in income would mean a decrease in food stamps which would leave hard-working people right where they started and unable to dig out. I knew the system was broken but I also knew that many families (eventually including my own) could not survive without it.

As the service ended, I turned to Tim, whose face revealed the same reaction I was having, and said, "We can never come back here."

I've said it many times throughout this story, but my husband was a stickler for following the Word, so based on the verses in Matthew concerning inner-body turmoil, he requested a meeting with the pastor and his wife. We thought, at best, we could understand each other a little better and at worst, we'd agree to disagree but leave on relatively good terms. It took much imploring. Much. And when we finally got together over dinner, it was clear that we were too far gone and they were tired of the thorn in their flesh and content to see us go.

It was really hard to hear, having watched my husband devote ten years of his life to this ministry. He'd bent over backwards to implement, promote, and support every time a new "best seller" would change the vision of the church. He went from building an evangelistic (kickass) choir fashioned after the Brooklyn Tabernacle to seeing the choir delegated to back up singers for the more modern worship team; from director of community groups, getting people out of the four walls and into their neighborhoods based on the Simple Church methodology, to making Sunday School the front door of the church based on somebody's book about something. I lose track. Anyway, it had only been the last two years or so that Tim had become less of a "party line" guy and more the "thorn in the flesh" by pushing the staff on issues of racial reconciliation and poverty. And so we left.

It was our neighbor and one of my dearest friends (who happened to live in Section 8 housing and by good fortune had not been sitting in church with me the day he went off on her kind) who walked up to the house one afternoon and asked to talk to us. She pulled out her Bible and said, "Maybe I'm wrong but if I read what this says in Ephesians, it don't matter where we have church as long as we're learning the Word and loving each other. Why can't we just have church right here and then maybe more people from the community will come?" It was decided and "Church under the Tree" was born. (Yes, it was our version of Church under the Bridge.) There's a bit more detail about that in another section.

Full time ministry was hard and we were constantly revamping based on the needs we saw, the response of the community, and the chaos of our own family. Neither of us felt comfortable self-promoting, and we decided early on to follow the George Mueller example for our finances. Basically, we would make our needs known to God and trust him to supply.

We were never fully funded.

The ministry fared better than our personal finances, but we essentially gutted our savings account in order to feed our family. It was clear that local missions was just not in the church's vocabulary. International missions was ultimate. American church planting was noble. Full-time investment in a bunch of poor people in the 'hood? *Eh, why don't you just keep your day job?*

Through it all and right up until the end there seemed to be just one thing that was missing. God. He didn't show up and he didn't show out. That's not to say that I never "felt" like he was there. There were times when maybe we were worshipping or when we were studying when I would've said I sensed his presence. But the power? There was no power. No transformations. No matter how fervently we prayed. No matter how hard we cried. No matter how deeply we believed that he could. No matter how boldly we proclaimed it. People did what people do. And aside from a few friends and occasional stories about the crazy white people on the corner, I wouldn't say we made much impact at all.

And so, you may be thinking, ends the ranting of a bitter old fool.

Well, I would take issue with that –I'm not so old. Seriously, it's just not about being mad or hurt or disappointed in people. Yes, all of that stuff happened and yes, it affected us deeply but it's not what broke us. Take us out the of "wounded soldier" box and please try to see the whole picture.

Free Will and the Community of Commiseration

"A good conversation always involves a certain amount of complaining. I like to bond over mutual hatreds and petty grievances."
    -Lisa Kleypas, *Christmas Eve at Friday Harbor*

It happened again today. I've been sitting in Starbucks several hours a day, several days a week for several months and I see it over and over. It's possible that I observe more of it because of my proximity to a large Baptist seminary, but even taking this into account it seems like a fairly accurate representation based on my thirty-plus years of experience. Frankly, it happens all the time. And every time I see it I have the same feelings I had the day I wrote this in my journal almost a year ago:

"I feel an unexpected sadness in regard to my Christianity (if that even remains a viable claim) and toward Christians in general. It's not pity or condescension but actual sorrow. I suddenly realize how much of our relationships, friendships, community, corporate gatherings, and even personal worship center around the commiseration of our failures. How many hours have I spent with dear friends alternating confession of our shortcomings, urging each other to deeper levels of repentance, and committing to "do better" next time? Countless.

We embrace this solemn shroud like a calling, our teaching and curriculum reflecting it: What if marriage is not meant to make you happy but holy? What if parenting is not meant to make us happy but holy? What is life itself is not meant to make us happy but holy? What of happiness? I don't mean the televangelist, plastic smile, plastered hair version but good old-fashioned happiness just... because. Well, true happiness only comes in the pursuit of obedience to the goal of holiness. But my Christian experience and education yield that the perpetual nature of sin makes the goal of holiness forever elusive and our pursuit of it futile. And so we commiserate."

Today it was two young ladies discussing their diets and plans to take better care of their "temples" while forking down their salads. One encouraged the other to take time every day to think about why she was choosing to eat healthier foods and how it would bring glory to God. The other stared at the table defeated. On another day, it was two guys berating themselves for wasting time watching television when they should be studying their Bibles and later, a couple of moms sighing deeply because they lost their temper with the little ones again.

Please know that I only mock them in so much as I was one of them. I am not morbidly obese, but like most women I struggle over those fifteen to twenty pounds that I could stand to lose. I prayed about it many times. I prayed for greater self-discipline (an ironic concept, don't you think?); I prayed that I would "hunger and thirst for righteousness" instead of sugar and carbs. I asked God to replace my thoughts of food with verses of Scripture and to turn my desire for cheesecake into a desire for the Word. I was serious. I was sincere just like these two ladies. But I can testify that Jesus never showed up to guard my refrigerator door, sucking his teeth with one eyebrow raised, shaming me back to the treadmill. Nope.

I've spent most of my entire adult life pushing for the elusive "daily quiet time" and repenting of laziness, poor priorities, or distractibility when I failed to live up to my own expectations. Goodness knows, I've agonized over parenting issues on every inch of the spectrum. Let's not even begin to talk about marriage.

During our time as youth pastors (I claim the title despite not having an official position or salary because I worked my ass off) we were going through the "True Love Waits" curriculum with our teenagers. I remember telling them that in a moment of temptation God would not magically appear and scream "Stop! Do not have sex!" This was why it was important that they make the decision before it got to that point.

They had to make the choice because God was not likely to interfere directly. If I wanted to have a consistent quiet time, I had to choose to set the alarm clock and drag myself out of bed. Don't want to overeat? Decide not to. Don't want to lose your temper? Decide not to. It all comes down to choices. My choices. Your choices. There's really nothing spiritual, let alone magical, about it, not for hormone crazed teens or for women battling the bulge. It's just a matter of choices.

But what about this crazy book? This Bible and these "promises"? If I really rejoiced in the Lord always and really brought my requests to him and let go of anxiousness and worry, would he really guard my heart and mind? Did I have to do it perfectly to reap the benefit? If even Paul said that he didn't always do the good things that he wanted to do and often ended up doing the bad things that he didn't want to do, isn't he the same as well, every human being that has ever lived? And if so, how could we ever distinguish the power of the Holy Spirit from just plain old human nature?

For the most part, Christians are not shaken up by these questions because, after all, they have the "doctrine of free-will" to fall back on. Quite simply put, this means that we have the freedom to choose obedient action or to choose disobedient action. And if we choose disobedient action (any action that is not in line with the will of God) we have no one to blame but ourselves. But exactly where do the two "wills" intersect? If I sincerely desire to choose obedience but lack the ability to make that choice autonomously, is there no obligation, or at the very least reasonable expectation, for intervention, empowerment, strengthening by the supposedly indwelling Holy Spirit?

Let me share a part of my testimony that I have never shared publicly before now. (Actually, I tried to share it once but was informed that "we pastor's wives can't be too open with people." Well, we "agnostic wives" will choose to be as open as we damn well please.) It's a very intimate topic but I think it best addresses the subject at hand.

As I explained, I grew up in a Christian home, but that's not to say it was without its challenges. Behind closed doors my father had an addiction to pornography. As a six year old, of course, I had no working knowledge of either of those two words: "addiction" or "pornography" - but what I did have was ample opportunity to view men and women on television doing things that for reasons I could not understand were very arousing to both my mind and my body. It wasn't long before this exposure yielded an addiction all my own – one of self-gratification, that is, masturbation.

By age eleven, I had seen every, EVERY sexual act that a man and woman (and various combinations of them) could perform with or to each other in living color. Stories ranging from married sex to adultery to one night stands, even violence and assault. Many of these images are forever burned into my brain and pop up when I least expect it.

Despite having given my heart and life to Jesus, I spent most of my childhood and teenage years doubting my salvation because of this one issue. Though I eventually came to believe that I wouldn't burn in hell for touching myself, I was still weighed down by this overwhelming guilt and shame - guilt and shame that I carried into my relationship with my husband. I entered the marriage bed expecting complete failure because I just knew that God was finally going to judge me - like He'd been saving it up and waiting for the perfect moment to nail my butt to the wall. A dysfunctional sex life was going to be my penance, if you will, for years of self-abuse.

Ten years of marriage and successful sex later, I finally considered the possibility that God was not waiting to rain down wrath on my head. I also decided that it was time to come clean with Tim and see if the two of us couldn't overcome some of my inhibitions together. Now, almost another ten years later, we are good. Really good, in case anyone's wondering, but that is far from the point.

The point is this: an eight year-old girl who by the lack of good judgment on the part of the adults in her life lays in bed at night consumed by a physical desire, fueled by any number of sounds and images seared in her mind's eye prays. And prays. And prays. She asks God to help her stop having "bad thoughts" and to take away the urge to "sin" and to help her sleep. Sleep doesn't come. She quotes the memory verses she's learned in Sunday school to keep her mind busy. It doesn't help. She hums the hymns that are familiar to her as a distraction. They don't distract. Eventually, she gives up. She touches herself because it feels good and because it's the only way she's going to get to sleep. Then she cries. She cries because she's embarrassed. She cries because she is guilty. She cries because she remembers the preacher saying that if you commit the same sin over and over, you probably aren't really saved. Then she cries because she's scared.

Lather. Rinse. Repeat. Time and again.

As an adult, I found myself sharing this story privately with many women over many random conversations. I, who was convinced that I was the only female on the planet plagued by what had long been dubbed a "boy issue," was flabbergasted as each one revealed their own similar struggle. Some, like me, had been exposed to varying degrees of inappropriate materials, but others had been completely sheltered from images of "immorality" and yet still found themselves in a cycle of desire and guilt. I grappled over the implication of this with a trusted friend.

"It's a sin." She offered definitively.

"But…"

"But nothing. If God's word says it's a sin then, it is."

I was at a bit of a loss and then I challenged her view of scripture with scripture itself.

"The word also says, 'There is no temptation so great that the Father has not made a way of escape.' As a child, where was my way of escape?" I asked.

"Obviously the adults in your life made poor judgments in their own sin issues but that doesn't mean that God failed you."

Okay. So, God did not fail me. He just allowed someone else's free-will and the stimulation of the natural sexual responses He created within my body to leave me weeping in fear of eternal damnation? *Yes, Jesus loves me?*

Similarly, I recently recalled one (of many) moments with my husband in which my daughter and I were locked in conflict over a lie. I knew she had done something but she absolutely refused to own up to it. We were standing on the back porch and I was completely exasperated by her level of deception and finally, I stopped speaking to her and just started praying in my mind. She had been baptized and we believed she'd made a sincere profession of faith, so it seemed reasonable to me that God could and should intervene. I asked the Holy Spirit to empower my daughter to be truthful. I wanted one word, just one truthful word from her mouth, as evidence that God was at work in her and that He was as vested in her overcoming these sin issues as I was. I was not just asking politely either. Inside I was screaming for help. I was quoting the Scripture that promised the power of the resurrected Christ was inside my daughter and was strong enough to break through this moment of stubbornness.

I pleaded with God to be faithful to His promise that "whatever you ask for in my name, I will do, so that the Father may be glorified in the Son." Surely, breaking the stronghold of lies in my daughter's life would bring glory to the Father. How could it not be His will for her to speak the truth when He is truth? I prayed for ten or fifteen minutes while she just stood there staring at the ground and I prayed with absolute faith that He not only could but would, had every reason to, answer my prayer. Finally, I asked her once again about the situation at hand. Once more, she lied. And I dropped my head in surrender and sadly wondered if my daughter's conversion had also been a deception. How else could I explain God's refusal to answer? The failure could not be on His part. It had to be her or me. Somehow one of us had quenched the spirit. Never mind fear, never mind abuse, never mind the default programming of a brain flooded by trauma. Somebody was a liar and it couldn't be God so… I not only regret this moment but years of following "biblical counsel" and the condemnation that did greater damage to my already wounded child.

And I would have to ask those who hold the Bible as inerrant and God as sovereign, but still commiserate over their horrible shortcomings…why? Why doesn't He answer? Specifically, if He is the all-knowing God as many purport He is, why would He remain silent, knowing that we would be driven down a path of absolute skepticism by our search for help that He Himself did not provide?

I saw a blog entry recently based on Psalm 50:15 which says "Call on me in a day of trouble; I shall rescue you and you will honor me." The blogger challenged that when we fail to call on God in our distress, we deny Him the opportunity to be faithful to this promise. If turnabout is fair play then I would have to wonder…when we DO call on Him in the day of trouble – desperately, and He DOES NOT rescue - has He not denied us the opportunity to "honor Him"? And why then should we bear the blame for that dishonor?

But we do. Somehow. And so we commiserate.

Sabbatical

> "No man ever believes that the Bible means what it says: He is always convinced that it says what he means."
>
> -George Bernard Shaw

By the end of 2011, we had been official missionaries under non-profit status for two years and while in some ways, Tim was hitting his stride, our family was flailing. My RAD daughter was giving us a run for our money and we were anxiously awaiting our first therapy session. We were homeschooling the oldest three kids, taking our eleven year old to weekly physical therapy appointments for developmental issues, entertaining the youngest two, and running our wannabe homestead while trying to create an example of creation stewardship for our community. Though we had recently discontinued the house church that met in our home for almost a year, Tim was still maintaining several small Bible studies in the neighborhood. We were worn out. Let me rephrase that... *I* was worn out. Frazzled. Sick. Depressed.

Tim was, to coin a phrase, righteously energized. Well, he was physically just as tired as the rest of us, so maybe righteously motivated would be more appropriate. Like so much of our life outlined in this book, Tim was driven by Scripture's mandate to make disciples. I was barely holding on to the "help-meet" notion while fighting my own health and stress levels and I'll be the first to admit that my husband's zeal created occasional conflict. Over the years we'd had plenty of heated discussions when I felt the kids and I were being slighted in the name of ministry. There were hitchhikers and homeless dudes that took precedent over movie night with the kids. There were even a few times when I felt our safety was put in jeopardy, but no matter what leverage I thought I had, Tim was always holding the trump card: Jesus. I mean seriously, when would the "you're an hour late for dinner" hand ever take the pot over the "I just shared the gospel with a former convict" that Tim was throwing down? Um, never.

Then came the board meeting that would change it all.

Our board of directors was hand-picked. Most of them had been part of our community work even before we were an official organization. They'd attended and chaperoned events in the 'hood, taken up collections for emergency needs, and helped us corral and supervise a dozen kids who attended church with us each week. In addition, there were the specific strengths each one brought to the table.

Robby, for example, aside from being a magnet for kids, full of energy and able to leap park benches in a single bound (shirtless if necessary), was also part of a new church plant team. He knew first-hand the stress of eking out a living from donations and the man hours required to build a community of believers from the ground up.

There was Jon, who is one of the most thoughtful and gracious men I've ever known. He and his wife were on track toward international missions and spent much time investing in the lives of refugees state-side. Jon understood both the cultural hurdles and blessing we would experience.

Lans was our plumb line, always measuring our ministry schedule against our family and marriage time. Of course, he was usually fighting a losing battle, but he did try. In addition, Lans and his wife, an interracial couple - with their seven children - knew well the unique personal challenges our family faced.

And then there was Francie. Her list of credentials could leave you feeling quite small and unaccomplished but her humility and sincere, unconditional support made you believe you were the most valuable human on the planet. Individually, they were friends: people we laughed with, vented to, and often tortured with sarcasm. As a board, we trusted their judgment, their wisdom, and their decisions implicitly.

On December 11th, prior to the meeting, Tim and I had spent much of the day in disagreement. He was settled on moving the ministry in a particular direction. I was overwhelmed by every possibility and felt lost in the process. We basically decided to move through the necessary agenda and leave the personal stuff to sort out later, but as we waited for all the members to call in on the conference number, our resident Barnabas, Francie, turned the tide with a simple question.

"So, while we are waiting, Amie, I would love to hear how you are doing. How are you taking care of yourself? What are your creative outlets and how are you getting recharged in the middle of being a wife and mom?"

Gulp. Personal stuff: front and center. I answered honestly. To summarize what became a very long meeting, the board suggested that we halt all ministry plans and take a six month sabbatical. For me, it was a welcomed relief, a chance to breathe, to create, to find myself under layers of fatigue; assuming there was something left to find. I really didn't care if it was biblical or not. It felt necessary. For Tim though, it was a punch to the gut. He had no idea how to reconcile the authority of the board with the authority of Scripture. In his mind, the two were in direct contradiction to each other. He was being told to "take a break" but saw no evidence of such in the Word. Sure, Jesus attempted a retreat every now and then but only to pray, and rarely with any success because He inevitably relented to the needs of the people. Tim was also being asked to not just put his family first, but for the next six months to make them the sole priority. While this is accepted as practical Christian living by most, it is not the example of Christ. (No. It's really not.) They were in essence giving us permission, or better yet instructing, Tim to live the life of nominal/normal Christianity. I was ready and willing by that point, while Tim agreed to the arrangement for my sake and in submission to this group of wise counselors. In the end, it would not have the effect everyone was expecting.

Tim quit reading his Bible. Completely. He was not being lazy. He was not angry with God. He was not "giving Satan a foothold." He was simply torn. He knew that if he read his Bible, as he had done practically every day of his life prior, he would immediately feel the stress of the conflict. He knew that he would read Jesus' words in Matthew:

"Anyone who loves his father or mother more than me is not worthy of me; anyone who loves his son or daughter more than me is not worthy of me; and anyone who does not take his cross and follow me is not worthy of me" (10:37-38).

"And everyone who has left houses or brothers or sisters or father or mother or children or lands, for my name's sake, will receive a hundredfold and will inherit eternal life." (19:29)

Or in Mark:

"Then Jesus' mother and brothers arrived. Standing outside, they sent someone in to call him. A crowd was sitting around him and they told him, 'Your mother and brothers are outside looking for you.' 'Who are my mother and my brothers?' he asked. Then he looked at those seated in a circle around him and said, 'Here are my mother and brothers! Whoever does God's will is my brother and sister and mother" (3:31-35).

Or even in Luke:

"If anyone comes to me and does not hate his father and mother, his wife and children, his brothers and sisters – yes even his own life -he cannot be my disciple" (14:26).

Oh, I can hear your gears turning, Christian friend.

But Amie…you and Tim just took everything way too literally. The only way those passages work while allowing you to focus on basic living and family interaction instead of truly forsaking your loved ones for the kingdom is if you *interpret them 1) according to your own context, or 2) spiritualize them, or 3) make them about the heart, or idols, or a mindset in which you acknowledge your <u>willingness</u> to give up everything for Christ <u>without actually doing so</u>…because that's just crazy.*

I think I can speak for both myself and my husband when I say, "No shit, Sherlock!" In fact, this is how the whole thing works. Each believer picks and chooses the verses that he/she will interpret as literal or metaphorical, universal or contextual, applicable or non-applicable. Tim and I leaned heavily on the literal side and took to heart (and put into action) the ideas of orphan care, racial reconciliation, social justice, charity, evangelism, and the pursuit of kingdom life here on earth. Others lean toward the spiritualized side and see only sin, redemption, and the eternal fulfillment of the kingdom.

It's this amazing thing labeled by Christian Smith in *The Bible Made Impossible*: Pervasive Interpretive Pluralism.

> "The very same Bible—which biblicists insist is perspicuous and harmonious—gives rise to divergent understandings among intelligent, sincere, committed readers about what it says about most topics of interest. Knowledge of "biblical" teachings, in short, is characterized by invasive interpretive pluralism.
>
> What that means in consequence is this: in a crucial sense it simply does not matter whether the Bible is everything that

> biblicists claim theoretically concerning its authority, infallibility, inner consistency, perspicuity, and so on, since in actual functioning the Bible produces a pluralism of interpretations."

In this vein of interpretive pluralism, there are also those who categorize believers in terms of legalism versus grace. But this is a self-serving oversimplification. After all, there are various commands that Christians simply expect other Christians to obey *quite* legalistically: don't commit murder, for example. To suggest that we created our own bondage under a generic label (as though we were pulling these ideas out of thin air) may put people's minds at ease and allow them to keep us safely in some non-self-incriminating box, but it's just not really fair.

Despite the lack of personal study time, we still loaded our crew up on Sunday mornings and headed to church. Given my skepticism about the sovereignty model I'd been taught, the long sought answers for our daughter's mental health issues, and now, the apparent incompatibility of our faith and our family life, church was the proverbial knot at the end of my rope.

Part Four: Sinking Sand

Yahweh Unraveled

> "Not that I am (I think) in much danger of ceasing to believe in God. The real danger is of coming to believe such dreadful things about Him. The conclusion I dread is not 'so there's no God after all,' but 'so this is what God's really like. Deceive yourself no longer.'"
>
> -C.S. Lewis, *A Grief Observed*

Lots of people have concluded that our loss of faith stems from our isolation from a local church body. In reality, we were almost never without a church family or without some "nourishment" from an outside source, so, before I delve into the topic of this section, I feel it's necessary to give you a bit of a timeline. For nearly two years after trading full-time paid ministry for full-time missions we continued to be an active part of the church we'd served in for many years. We attended both worship services and Sunday School, which Tim taught, usually with six to twelve neighborhood kiddo's in tow. It wasn't until concerns regarding political views and stereotypes that seemed contrary to the nature of our mission work became blaringly obvious that we separated ourselves from that congregation. We talked it over with some of those who'd been attending church with us from our neighborhood and decided that we would simply follow the biblical pattern for church as it existed in the book of Acts.

We playfully dubbed ourselves "church under the tree" in reference to the large willow tree under which we held "services" each Sunday. We met, not only for study, but shared a meal together every week as well. It was a great time of learning both from the word and from life lived together in very challenging ways. We represented different families, different histories, different cultures, different styles of worship, and even different tastes in food. There was no lack for stress, no lack of differences in opinions, and no lack of humble pie to be eaten (much of it by yours truly). But there was much laughter, much to learn, and much love shared (if you don't count the playful fighting over who got to hold the two new babies that were born that year). There was sweetness to the reality of it that I still appreciate today. After a time though, we were weary and some of our younger members grew more and more distracted during study times and it began to feel like church as usual, which was never the goal. We disbanded the group in favor of a new discipleship study that was being used in foreign mission fields and was less literary-based and more story-based, which was better suited for our demographic.

During this time our family started attending a small church in a neighboring town. We were about two months into our sabbatical when the church began a study on the book of First Samuel. As I've already shared, sovereignty had become an unsettling issue for me. Unfortunately, you can't study the Old Testament with its laws, wars, plagues, etc. without slamming right into the all-powerful though often contradictory will of God. Sure enough, it was only a matter of weeks before we came across the first hurdle.

In the second and third chapters of this book, we find the story of Eli. For those who don't know, Eli is a priest and is given charge over Samuel who would eventually become God's mouthpiece to King Saul. But Eli had problems - sons, that is - who were also priests but were corrupt. Because of their wickedness, God declares judgment against Eli and his entire household; neither Eli nor any man from his lineage would live to see old age.

As we reviewed the text that day in church, there was a question of blame, well…responsibility. Was it simple rebellion on the part of these boys that brought down God's wrath? Was it poor judgment and permissive parenting by Eli? Or was it some combination of the two? There was a lot of bantering back and forth and plenty of exhortation regarding our own parenting and accountability before God on behalf of our children. Having been vicariously trained by my husband's seminary education, I was scouring the passages before and after to get a full view of the context. It was then that I noted a verse we had skipped right over in our study. In verse twenty-five of chapter one, we find that Eli did in fact confront his sons regarding their behavior. The verse concludes with these words:

>"Nevertheless, they did not heed the voice of their father, because the Lord desired to kill them."

I raised my hand, read the verse aloud, and proposed that maybe no one was to blame. My question was not whether

God purposing to kill was right or wrong (that would come later) but whether we were willing to entertain the notion, to lay blame where it appeared to belong. The interpretive gymnastics began almost immediately.

"We don't know if the word 'desire' means the same thing to God as it does to us."

Another:

"Kill' in the original language may translate differently."

And another:

"It could just mean that God knew they would not listen and therefore He knew they would have to be killed."

I left that day wondering why it always seemed necessary to have four commentaries, a Bible dictionary, and a working knowledge of ancient languages to read God's "love letter" to me. Or at least to keep it from saying what it seemed to be saying.

Several chapters later we came to another crisis of sovereignty. In the fifteenth chapter, Samuel (all grown up now) instructs Saul with "the words of the Lord" to attack the city of Amalek. Specifically he is told to:

"Utterly destroy all that they have, and do not spare them. But kill both man and woman, infant and nursing child, ox and sheep, camel and donkey" (15:3)

Why? Why did the Amalekites of every age deserve to die? Because their ancestors some three hundred years earlier attacked the Israelites on their way out of Egypt. *Three hundred* years earlier. Controversy over the historical evidence of the Jewish exodus aside, this would be akin to Great Britain blowing the Unites States off the map in about sixty years. Seven and a half generations later, my great-grandkids would finally get what they deserve for that whole "revolutionary war" nonsense. Crazy as all that sounds, it's not even the point.

The point is the mental acrobatics and compartmentalization we are willing to do to justify the seemingly unjust actions of our Old Testament deity. This time it was our pastor who raised the obvious question.

"So, God just ordered the destruction of an entire people group. Does anyone have a problem with this?" he asked.

At first it was crickets. I sat on my hands, my toe tapping feverishly as I fought for restraint. Then came the responses: interpretation/translation confusion, the "original language" barrier, all the usual suspects. One person summarized it by saying, "God's word is to be obeyed no matter what." Inside I was yelling: Easy for you to say, you haven't been asked to murder your neighbor's new born baby!

Slowly, I raised my hand, a sight the pastor was no doubt beginning to dread, and offered my observation.

"We had a serious problem with this sort of thing on September 11, 2001."

Whether the intention behind my comment was understood or not, I can't say. Regardless, the study continued in a "trust and obey" direction. Tim and I discussed it further on the way home. What credibility did we have to condemn Muslim followers for exacting vengeance on the "infidels" according to the teaching of Allah, when our own Yahweh was commanding the same thing right there in black and white? By what standard could we definitively condemn one while blindly defending the other? I was still fighting to "keep the faith" but found it harder and harder to stifle the doubts.

This was the Sunday I told Tim that I felt our church attending days were coming to a close. I didn't feel like I could be true to myself by squelching the barrage of questions that surfaced as we studied, but I also had no desire to be the resident skeptic. Regardless of the inner struggle, the people of this congregation had been good to us. They welcomed us, loved on our kids, and trusted us with our daughter's condition in ways prior communities had fallen short. They were coming together each week for their own spiritual refreshment, not to deal with a detractor. I have always hoped they knew that we didn't leave because of them but for their sakes. This was our journey and I didn't feel comfortable taking them along involuntarily. But as I stated at the beginning on this section, we were not the proverbial "lump of coal" taken out of the fire pit and left alone to cool and harden as illustrated by countless pastor's across the land. We were always trying to maintain Christian community and participation in a local body just as the scriptures instructed.

Even so, the thread which had been loosed during my son's illness was now beginning to collect in a pile on the ground as the fabric of my faith hung in frayed loops. The final tug came from an unexpected source.

We subscribe to Netflix via our Wii. It's one of the only "non-necessity" charges we incur each month, but with five kids and a weekly family movie night, it's cheaper than the rental box. (This is especially true when you notoriously return the movies late.) Besides access to some of our favorite sit-coms, we have absolutely loved the documentaries and foreign films. I have however, learned a few things, thanks to this service.

Number one –I am horrible at choosing movies. Many of mine and Tim's in-home date nights have included us staring at each other, perplexed by the dark, twisted, or downright stupid plot of my film choice.

Number two –All British movies involve someone being hit by a car at a most unexpected moment. How do I know this? See "number one".

Movies are funny things. They are all meant to draw some emotion from us: fear, laughter, nostalgia, love. And really, it's not that hard. We are highly emotive creatures, easily manipulated thanks to our knack for empathy and nature as social beings. Did you cry at the end of "E.T."? Did you fight to stay awake all night after "Nightmare on Elm Street"? Did you smile with devilish satisfaction when Julia Roberts delivered the line, "Come quickly. I've just killed an intruder" in "Sleeping with the Enemy"? Damn right, you did. Granted, I've just aged myself, but substitute any of your favorite sci-fi, thriller, horror, romance movies and the result is the same. Movies affect us.

Then there are the ones that rock your very soul. They settle into your bones and ache there for awhile. You have your own list, I'm sure. Mine includes epic productions such as "Glory," "Dances with Wolves," and "Schindler's List," and then the one which, for me, drove the nail in Yahweh's coffin: "The Story of Soraya M."

I read the Netflix summary with the understanding that it would detail the potential stoning of a woman unjustly accused of adultery. Potential. Possible. This is what I understood. Only minutes into the movie it was evident that this was not a "what might happen" movie but a "what did happen" story. I paused it and placed my hand on Tim's shoulder, feeling the need to steady myself.

"They are going to kill this woman." Tim nodded. "I just need to say it out loud so my brain can prepare itself."

We restarted the movie and I sat unblinking for the next two hours, occasionally swallowing the pit of nausea that crept from my gut to the back of my throat. I often tell people if they would like to experience the movie without actually watching it they should simply rip their heart out of their chest, stomp the hell out of it, and shove it in again. Same difference.

But if the acting, the horrible, nagging "based on a true story" knowledge, or the unfathomable injustice were not enough to destroy me, there would still be the last few lines. As Zahra, the Muslim woman sharing the story of her niece's unjust, horrific death puts herself between the men of town who are responsible and the car of the journalist who goes on to tell the world about it, she throws her arms out and cries:

"What are you afraid of? Isn't our God good?"

The words pierced me. Others may perceive them differently but to me they were dripping with poignant sarcasm. While her devotion to Allah is made clear throughout the movie, it is their use of God to carry out such corruption that she calls into question. If God is good, then surely their actions were just and they had no reason to fear exposure.

The issue I suddenly could not reconcile was man's inclination to justify acts done by or in the name of "God" while simultaneously condemning the actions of other religious groups. It was like the Samuel Bible study all over again. How quickly we declared the attacks of September 11th on the World Trade Center to be unconscionable and the idea that these men believed they were following the instruction of their god, Allah, to be utterly absurd and nonsensical. But isn't Yahweh-ordained annihilation of enemies evidenced throughout the Old Testament? And while most of us would without question deem stoning to be inhumane, especially within the context of Muslim radicalism, don't we find the same punishment instituted by Yahweh in Deuteronomy 22:22? Not only in the instance of adultery, but rape as well. That's right. If a woman was raped inside the town and did not scream loud enough to draw rescuers then she was to be stoned to death. I guess Yahweh somehow missed the fight, flight, or freeze response system that he supposedly created or the apparently less than obvious fact that a man who is capable of overpowering a woman in order to assault her is probably also capable of stifling her cries. No need to bother with these little details. *Isn't our God good?*

As the dividing line between Yahweh, whom I'd considered my God all these years, and Allah, whom I'd easily dismissed as the fictional deity of a deceived people, became virtually indistinguishable, the tears that started in sorrow for this woman, Soraya, and her story became personal grieving for the loss of the God I had claimed as my own. Even if he wasn't quite dead to me, I would have to completely redefine him, which was the same difference.

Days later, while still processing the movie and all its complications, I experienced a proverbial "salt in the wound" moment. According to my Christian teaching, this woman who'd lived a life of abuse and suffered a horrendous, unjust, excruciating death, closed her eyes to this life only to be ushered into an eternity of more conscious torment because the unfortunate geography of her birthplace did not afford her the "correct" religious worldview.

How could it be that the sense of justice I had long believed to be a reflection of God in me was so overwhelmingly assaulted by His own system? Perhaps I had created God in my own image after all. Perhaps we were all doing the same.

Perhaps he was created from the beginning.

Two Paths, One Journey

> "Ye'll tak' the high road and I'll tak the low road
> And I'll be in Scotland afore ye…"
>
> -Author Unknown, *The Bonny Banks of Loch Lomond*

Having started our relationship in high school, Tim and I have practically grown up together. We have much in common and many of our views were forged under the same fire and with the same result. But I fear that some will think I have simply been "riding his coattails" or worse that I am the hand-wringing little woman trying to stand by my man while he goes off the deep end. I'm also certain there are at least a few who espouse the notion that I have led Tim by the nose into this place of rebellion. Make no mistake, Tim and I may be "one flesh" but we are different people capable of thinking and acting independently of one another. My study and understanding of scripture were all my own and often went in different directions from Tim's seminary-informed interpretations. We spent countless hours talking over every issue of this transition. Some we argued over; many, we cried over. I like to say that we ended up on the same page even though we were reading different books.

While Tim spent a lot of time researching in-depth, academia-type books on every range of belief/disbelief by authors such as Scott McKnight, N.T. Wright, Michael Dowd, John Loftus, Christopher Hitchins, Richard Dawkins, Christian Smith, etc., I was not quite ready to engage the intellectual depths most of these guys were covering. Also, I didn't want to give anyone the easy excuse of saying I started filling my mind up with other people's ideas.

To the contrary, I refused to read anything. Not a single book for or against Christianity. Not even the Bible, which only seemed to create more anxiety than answers. Instead, I decided to go straight to the Source. I prayed. I asked, implored, beseeched, pleaded with, and begged God to show Himself, to be as real to me as he was in any of the Sunday school stories I'd built my life around. I needed the fourth man in the fiery furnace, the burning bush, the sealed mouth of the lions, the parted waters, the writing on the wall, the angel, the vision…pick a miracle, any miracle, but I needed it to be evident - not some coincidence of timing or networking or natural consequence. If it was true that I had been worth saving, I needed to know that I was worth keeping.

Months passed.

Get a Job

> "Say something, I'm giving up on you
> I'm sorry that I couldn't get to you
> Anywhere I would've followed you
> Say something, I'm giving up on you."
>
> **A Great Big World -*Say Something***

A dear friend at the time told me in no uncertain terms that I had no right to ask anything of God. The mere fact that he had willingly redeemed my wretched soul from the pit of hell was more than he ever owed me and more than I deserved, and any expectation beyond that was an effort to manipulate God, and that I wasn't really disappointed in God but in his refusal to be my puppet. Maybe you agree with her sentiment.

My response was (and is) simply this: if it was God who called me his child and co-heir with Jesus his son (Galatians 4:7) and whose word declared him my "Abba, daddy" (Romans 8:15) and who said (in his incarnational state) that I could ask anything in his name and he would do it (John 14:13-14) then I had every fucking right.

Surely any parent can understand this perspective. If your child cries out "Daddy!" in fear or pain in the middle of the night, which of you stands by with arms crossed thinking, *' How dare you try to control me with your manipulative, desperate tears? I'm not your puppet. You just sit there alone in the dark until you learn to trust me more."*? That is crazy. And the child who is parented this way would suffer irreparable trauma and require extensive help to learn to trust again. I know this all too well. Can we not expect at least the same effort from a heavenly father that we expect from any decent human father?

How you would answer that last question is mostly irrelevant now. The answer never came.

It was nearing the end of summer when the same friend who rebuked me for expecting God to reveal himself to me in a real way sent me several messages. She knew that I was trying to avoid taking in new information, either for or against Christianity, but she urged me to make an exception and read the book of Job. We had shared years of friendship and honest exchange and so, because she asked me to, I agreed.

I don't actually know what she thought or hoped I would get from reading Job. I knew the story, of course, and figured it had something to do with Job's refusal to turn his back on God no matter how crappy his life got. Maybe it was just a biblical example to confirm her previous declaration that God is not to be questioned and to convince me likewise. I assume that was the goal, but it was not the result.

Let me share some of my thoughts about Job. Yes, I read it. Completely. Again. Not only that but I also checked out a book from the library on it: *The Book of Job: When Bad Things Happened to a Good Person* by Harold S. Kushner - which was absolutely wonderful, by the way.

As a literary work, I think the book of Job is amazing. It reminds me so much of a Shakespearean play. The prologue sets the stage, followed by a series of dramatic, opposing monologues which build to the final act and resolution. Brilliant.

As a literal occurrence in the history of mankind as deemed by literal Biblicists, however, I find more problems than solutions. Still, I went into it with an open mind; if the silver bullet was in there, I wanted to find it. I got all the way to verse six.

> "Now there was a day when the sons of God came to present themselves before the Lord, and Satan also came among them."

Wait a second, the sons of God…and Satan also. What?

It only got worse from there. Satan and God have a rather chummy conversation over the condition of Job's faith, resulting in the unfortunate loss of Job's five hundred donkeys, five hundred oxen, seven thousand sheep, three thousand camels, seven sons, and three daughters to thieves, fire, and a great wind. All within minutes of each other. Sounds like a classic soap opera plot doesn't it? Cue music and hold camera seven on Job's anguished expression for three, two…

Or not.

> "…and he (Job) fell on the ground and worshiped" (1:20).

Huh? Surely the author meant to say cried or screamed or bawled or kicked and flailed in agony, right? Because these are the natural human responses to tragedy (much less tragedy thousands of times over). Worshiped? Really?

I remember the day we learned that one of our dear friends had passed away unexpectedly. He was an amazing man and musician who'd worked with us on several of my would-be-songwriter projects. We were out of state visiting family and Tim pulled me aside and gave me the news. My first words were, "Holy shit!" - my thoughts immediately going to his wife and children. Absolute heartbreak.

On Facebook that day, one person shared a very different reaction. She said, "When I heard that he was gone, my very first thought was 'oh how wonderful that he's in heaven with Jesus.'"

When I read this tidbit that day, I can tell you that I did not at any point think to myself, "Wow, she is such a righteous soul and so very much like Job who worshipped in the midst of utter despair." Nope. It was more along the lines of "what a bitch!"

I know there are people who hold up well under pressure, but I have a hard time believing that a stoic submission to sovereignty when faced with devastating trauma is anyone's authentic self, and it only furthers my belief that Job was a fictional character.

But even if you lay aside the extremity of Job's reaction to suffering which lends to its mythological feel and ignore the verses in which God seems to take credit for Job's demise or the verses which imply polytheism - or any other questions concerning the text itself - I still didn't understand how this was supposed to convince me that asking God to speak for Himself was off-limits. Especially, when half the book is Job's pleading for answers from God.

"Therefore I will not keep silent; I will speak out in the anguish of my spirit, I will complain in the bitterness of my soul." (7:11)

"If I have sinned, what have I done to you, O watcher of men? Why do you not pardon my offenses and forgive my sins?" (7:20 & 21)

"…I desire to speak to the Almighty and to argue my case with God." (13:3)

"Though he slay me, yet will I trust Him. *Even so*, I will defend my own ways before him." (13:15, Italics mine)

For all of Job's righteousness and faithfulness, he never stopped saying "Please explain yourself. Please just let me off the hook here. If it's me, tell me and I'll own it, but if it's just you, please help me understand."

Naturally, the argument to follow would be that God answered Job by essentially saying, "Can it, mister. I'm in control here!" At long last, God challenges Job with a series of "Did you…Can you…Were you…Will you…Do you know…?" questions and Job relents.

Of course he did. We all know this tactic works. When my kids sass me over basic chores and responsibilities I can get very um, god-like, in an instant.

"*Do you know* who you are talking to? *Did you* pay the house payment this month? *Are you* going to work tomorrow? *Will you* be buying groceries from now on?"

They shut up almost immediately, more likely due to annoyance over my ranting than because of my compelling logic. Maybe that's why Job finally cries uncle. Maybe not.

The greater point is, regardless of the answer, there was an answer. And I was willing to be told to "shut up" by God. I was willing to break out the dust and ashes. I knew what was at risk if I asked God to show up. I also knew what was at risk if I didn't ask at all.

More time passed and no answer came.

Part Five: Climbing Out

Amendment One Undone

> "**Doubt grows with knowledge.**"
> -Johann Wolfgang von Geothe

I have often said that God never allowed us a conviction He didn't force us to live up to. If the Bible taught that adoption was close to the Father's heart, five adopted kids were proof in the pudding. If Paul's ministry reflected intentional racial reconciliation, then lip-service was not enough. Instead, those adopted children would be black, bi-racial, and Haitian and would allow us opportunities to "break down the walls of hostility." If Jesus blessed the poor, touched the lepers, kept company with prostitutes, and dined with thieves, then moving into the 'hood, sheltering gangsters, praying with exotic dancers, and sharing Thanksgiving dinner with registered pedophiles made perfect sense to us. Yep. It was apparent that God had us on a "put your money where your mouth is" plan. Strangely, it didn't seem there were many of us on that plan. In fact, some were downright hostile to it.

"Because you are moving into a poor neighborhood, does that mean the rest of us have to?" asked one pastor. Of course not! was the appropriate answer, but perhaps you can see how this type of scrutiny added fuel to our frustration with the local church. The irony being that we were asking very similar questions ourselves: If Jesus does x, y, or z, do we have to do the same thing? Of course! was our answer, given the whole "be Christ-like" theme of the New Testament.

All of this to say, it was no big surprise when we bought a home right next door to a lesbian. While I maintained the fundamentalist view that homosexuality was sinful, I had long been convinced that we (the church) were winning no wars for the faith with our judgmental dogma. I was the one wondering why the church was protesting Gay Pride events when we should be passing out free water and saying "Jesus loves you" because well, He does, right? The following is a small portion of a spoken word that I wrote several years ago:

>from "Tempted to Love"
>Amie Sexton ©2009
>
>
>Would I see the homosexual as a formidable foe?
>Quickly hoisting a sign to make certain they know
>That my "God hates fags!"
>Oh, really. Is that so?
>
>And if it were true that God hates these "fags"
>Upon which of your sins do you suppose He gags?
>Is it the gossip that spews from your lips with ease
>Or bitterness that grows like a cancerous disease?
>
>Do we think their deeds more heinous than our own?
>That apart from His grace we could dare face His throne?
>Or could we halt our disgust long enough to explore
>The soul that's within, perhaps searching for more?

> If for once we could see them the way Jesus does
> Maybe seeing them truly, we'd be tempted to love.

Once again it seemed God was taking me to task. Here was my chance to put feet to my faith, walk the talk, practice what I preach, (enter your favorite cliché here).

It was harder than I thought it would be. Not because of her sexual orientation but because she was so stinking quiet. We had a few necessary neighborly conversations, but otherwise, she pretty much kept to herself - a defense mechanism that she'd probably learned the hard way. Her then two year-old son, on the other hand, was a chubby little bundle of chattiness, and when summer came and he took to letting himself in my back door, his mom and I got to know each other pretty quickly. It turned out we had a lot in common – we liked coffee when it tasted more like hot chocolate, both loved Mexican food (this would bond us for years and years), and we were both right smack in the middle of parenting insanity.

Contrary to what others may expect, there was no elephant in the room. Each of us knew where the other stood on the obvious issue. She never made me feel obligated to hide my beliefs, and in fact, would ask for relationship advice based on my understanding of the Bible. I figured that regardless of the context, the basic principles of love, respect, and faithfulness were applicable and shared them with her. I hoped that I never made her feel obligated to be anything less than herself. We chatted once about this very thing (over Mexican food, of course). I wanted to be sure that my perception of our relationship was based on reality and that I hadn't been a complete ass to her, having rewritten history in my own favor so, I asked and she reassured me with her response:

"If I had ever felt like you were judging me, I wouldn't be sitting at this table with you right now."

Of course, "loving my neighbor as myself" was one thing; coming to understand, respect, validate, and advocate for her lifestyle would take stepping out of the fundamentalist bubble and seeing reality un-skewed and bigotry unmasked.

The battle over same-sex marriage was fully ablaze in spring of 2012 in the great state of North Carolina. The upcoming Republican Primary would include on its ballot (don't even get me started on the clear political gerrymandering) Amendment One defining marriage as between one man and one woman. Living a stone's throw from a Baptist seminary, my husband's alma mater, you can already assume the direction much of our community was campaigning. "Vote for Amendment One" signs were everywhere. Despite the fact that I wasn't quite ready to take homosexuality off the chopping block of "unnatural affection" according to my Baptist upbringing, I was not about to contribute to a clear infringement on human rights or stand by as many of my Christian friends did just that in the name of the very Jesus who always sided with the outcast. It seemed to me that the church was claiming a defense of biblical standards - but only where this one deviation was concerned. I challenged what I saw as blatant hypocrisy in a blog post titled "To the Polls". Here is an excerpt:

"If conservative Christians are, as they purport to be doing, protecting God's biblical definition of marriage and thereby speaking on His behalf at the polls, then why aren't we formulating, marketing, and pushing through legislation to protect God's biblical sensitivities regarding ALL sexual acts? Why, in heaven's name, stop with a marriage amendment?

Come on Amie, grace has to supersede law at SOME point.

Ah yes, His grace is sufficient. Our constitution? Not so much, I guess.

Well, you can't expect the democratic government of a free and richly diverse people such as America to legislate every point of Christian morality. That would be legalism at its worst and set us back 200 years to a pre-revolutionary state church existence and would make it nearly impossible to follow Christ's command to show love, given the extremity of the law, constant mutual suspicion and condemnation, as well as the likelihood that none could escape its judgments thanks to that darned "all have sinned" thing.

Oh, how I love when these conversations go right where I want them to. ;-) You are right. And what's more it would be impossible because the line of morality among Christians is as variant as the day is long and is most often drawn just inside of one's own level of comfort.

So INSTEAD ---

Perhaps we should remember that the Constitution of the United States is not Scripture. And that there may be evidences of MANY sacred writings from MANY cultures and belief systems reflected in its content. But rights should never have been, and should never again, be afforded us by our common religion, or common race, or common gender, or common sexuality--but by our common humanity.

Instead, ask yourself "why do we draw the line here and not there?" "Here" being Amendment One and "there" being the Nth degree of the "biblical" standard. And if, in fact, you're not willing to push the line "there" then you have no choice but to unwrap the cause from its spiritual packaging with Bible-verse-quoting ribbons and bows and see that what you are left with is hypocrisy and discrimination. Stop dressing it up and putting God's name on the gift tag."

You can accuse me of many things, but shying away from controversy should not be one of them. I couldn't let go of the parallels between this movement and the anti-miscegenation laws which were not overturned until the late sixties and were also heavily justified as biblical. I could imagine the same visceral disgust and hostility toward homosexuals having been expressed at the sight of a mulatto child, my child, if born a mere forty-five years earlier. When would we ever learn from our mistakes?

As my heart was already sensitive to "justice for all," it was only a matter of time and research before I came to the obvious conclusion that homosexuality is not a sin issue. Watching the documentary featuring Dr. Tiger Devore regarding Disorders of Sexual Development (DSD) entitled "Me, My Sex, and I" left me shameful of the years of perpetuating black and white answers to an issue whose spectrum was, appropriately enough, as colorful as a rainbow. I remember calling Tim over to the computer where I was viewing the film and with tears in my eyes, all I could say was "We have been so wrong."

In the same way my daughter's "sins" were absolved in light of scientific evidence, so the stigma of homosexuality as sin was shattered. How is it possible that we can indisputably know that gender itself holds innumerable variations (i.e. intersex or ambiguous genitalia) and yet still maintain that sexual attraction is isolated to two norms? If your only argument is to quote Romans chapter one, let me remind you that Paul was not privy to the medical advances and research of our present day and could not have based his interpretation of homosexual behavior on anything other than his own preference OR… the views of the Old Testament writers who would have had even less understanding of the intricacies of the human body/psyche than did Paul. And if your follow up argument is that the authors were penning the inspired word of an all-knowing God, please consider that the same all-knowing deity apparently saw no reason to "inspire," much less inform, these same authors in basic scientific knowledge now universally accepted such as the fact that, oh, I don't know, washing your hands will stop the spread of germs.

Human sexuality is as vast a study as any in the medical/scientific community and it is irresponsible to condemn homosexuality based on the view held in a history book. The fundamentalist claims seem all-out illogical and individually incongruent unless you are the rare person who continues in this day and age to forego antibiotics in favor of leeching. In that case, I would at least be willing to appreciate your consistency.

Now, I stand alongside my lesbian friends, gay friends, bi-sexual friends, transgender friends, queer friends –not *in spite* of their sexual orientation but because of it. In acceptance of it. In celebration of it. And in defense of it! Oh, and I still teach my children what to look for in a mate. I tell them to look for someone who is kind, thoughtful, loving, tender, honest, full of integrity, intelligent, and hard-working. *That* person is a worthy candidate, regardless of ethnicity or gender.

WWJD *or What With Jesus Do*?

> **"Whether one believes in a religion or not, and whether one believes in rebirth or not, there isn't anyone who doesn't appreciate kindness and compassion."**
>
> **-Dalai Lama, *Kindness, Clarity, and Insight***

Sooner or later, I began reading a few books. I started with some liberal Christian authors. I had several liberal or progressive Christian friends who shared many of my views practically and politically but still maintained a framework of faith and a devotion to Christ, so I thought maybe that would work for me.

Up to this point, I had done some pretty impressive dancing around the Jesus part of the equation. Oh, you noticed I hadn't mentioned him much? Exactly. I had already decided that Yahweh was dead to me (or needing to be redefined in so many terms that it was the same as being dead), and the institutional church held no soft spot for me (not saying all persons, just the collective organization) but Jesus was…well, Jesus.

I had believed in God, reverenced him, and feared him rightly most days, but I *loved* Jesus. There is a reason these are essentially the first words of this story *and* nearing the last chapter of this book. Choosing not to believe in an invisible deity is hard enough after years of indoctrination; choosing to stop loving another person after years of devotion is really complicated. People kept asking me "What do you with Jesus?" and I kept saying "I don't know yet," but I knew I had to figure it out. I mean, he was God's son and said things like "I and the Father are one," which intricately connected him to Yahweh, whom I had no desire to resurrect (pun intended). He also said a lot of really bizarre things about Gehenna/hell/Hades and eternal consequences.

But he was the martyr on the cross, the one who touched lepers, who healed lame and blind, and defended women against a hypocritical patriarchal system. He overturned the economic exploitation of the religious "haves" even as he turned the money changers table over in the temple. He was passionate, compassionate, sympathetic, empathetic, and a little bit sarcastic by my take. His was the "greatest story ever told," but was he entirely unique?

One book that stopped me in my tracks was Marcus Borg's "Jesus and Buddha: The Parallel Sayings." I was astounded by the similarities in their lives, teachings by one that were almost verbatim of the other, and a common sense of ethereal divinity. But I was also disturbed, given that these two men/prophets and there represented religions were in no way comparable, according to fundamentalist teaching. One was objectively right and one objectively was wrong. Yet, here they were sharing the same wisdom, the same observations, five hundred years apart. How?

I had a pretty good idea how Christians would explain this (based on how I had been taught to explain common threads in various religions) and after several conversations, I was proven right. The basic reasoning is because Satan masquerades as an angel of light. He creates deceptively close imitations of the "real thing" in order to perpetuate confusion. So what this suggests, in the case of Buddha, is that Satan had intimate knowledge into the life of Christ, literally word for word, some five hundred years before Jesus existed. Okay…so how did God's arch nemesis get his hands on the script? Did he order it online? Did God leave his diary lying around and Satan happened upon it? Were they out for drinks one night and God got a little loose-tongued while Satan scribbled down notes on a napkin? Talk about perpetuating confusion!

Another possibility (and the one which I tend to hold) is that maybe there are universal principles, be they attributed to a specific god or not, which permeate history and are incorporated into many belief systems. And maybe that common thread points to the bigger picture, which whoever or whatever god is, is really trying to communicate. This idea pointed me in a new direction on this journey. I'd been wallowing around in the muck of what I didn't believe for so long. Now, I was ready to start considering what I *did* believe, and this idea of recurring themes seemed like a pretty good place to start.

Did you know that the "Golden Rule" is not a Christian idea? That it didn't originate in the Bible? Maybe you already knew that; you're probably smarter than I am. I'm glad to say that I know it now, but that wasn't always the case. I really thought that this was a uniquely Christian teaching. For most of my life I thought this way. Naïve, but true.

In reality the ethic of reciprocity can be found as far back as the Middle Kingdom of ancient Egypt some sixteen hundred to two thousand years before Christ, and it is reflected in every major world religion and most of the minor ones, too. It could be said, in terms of the universal principles, that this is the kingpin, the launch pad for all basic morality and humanity. And it resonated deeply within me. First, because it was not a foreign concept. It was exactly what drew me to Jesus in the first place: his sympathetic and empathetic nature, his care and attention to the least of these, his constant call to treat people with the same extent of justice washed in grace we desire for ourselves. The story of the woman caught in adultery is a prime example (even if this story may not have been in the original text). "You who are without sin cast the first stone," Jesus said. In other words, go ahead if you're willing to do to her what you would never want done to you.

This platform of morality also connected with my heart because it had been central to every part of ministry I'd ever participated in – adoption, social justice, charity and service to the poor - a constant drawing to the marginalized of society. And unlike many of the easily manipulated teachings of the Bible, it was such an easy concept. No, not always easy to do, but easy to measure in myself, easy to detect in others, easy to teach and worthy of being taught.

There is a common misnomer among believers that apart from God (specifically the god of the Bible), there is no behavioral code, that all atheists are without a moral compass, but here we find a consensus for basic human interaction throughout time and reflected in various and divergent faiths which would suggest otherwise.

So, what do I do with Jesus? In the end, I had to admit that the person of Christ, just like the Bible and God, was subject to individual interpretation. Even Jesus gets created in *our* image. Those who see him in a strictly redemptive role tend to spiritualize, if not trivialize, his teachings on poverty, economics, and kingdom living. Those who see him as an inclusive humanitarian tend to overlook that it was Jesus who introduced the concept of "wheat and tares," the "us versus them," "ingroup/outgroup" mentality. And those who see him as the great conqueror of evil willingly brandish his name and image to support their incessant spewing of condemnation and judgment. Will the real Jesus please stand up?

For this reason, I don't pray to him. I don't worship him. I don't claim to know his take on anything and I don't feel bound by what I thought I knew of him. Some days I hate him. I hate the some of the choices I made because of him. I hate my own interpretation of him and I hate everyone else's as well. Other days, I would still like to emulate certain things I saw in him.

And every now and then, I just miss him. Because I really did love him.

Whoever he was.

Sacred Pain

> "A miscarriage is a natural and common event. All told, probably more women have lost a child from this world than haven't. Most don't mention it, and they go on from day to day as if it hadn't happened, so people imagine a women in this situation never really knew or loved what she had.
>
> But ask her sometime: how old would your child be now? And she'll know."
> -Barbara Kingsolver

As of my writing of this book, there are only a handful of people who know what I am about to share. By the time you read it, there will be a handful more: those who deserved to hear it directly from us personally and not in sterile black and white ink.

There are certain types of pain which are sacred and want to be held in a safe place for a time until ready to be exposed to the light of day and processed within a greater community. Of course, not every loss has this luxury. In this society, most of our grieving is done very well within the public eye and often, shamefully, in a hurried and scheduled fashion. But some loss happens without any fanfare and in painful but necessary privacy. Here is an excerpt from my journal on Saturday, August 31, 2013:

To miscarry. To carry improperly? To handle incorrectly? It all sounds like you did something wrong.

"The quarterback throws a hail Mary with seconds left on the clock. The Sextons are wide open in the end zone. The baby ball is headed straight for them! This could be one for the history books, Joe. And they…they…they FUMBLED IT! Oh, my goodness, I can't believe it! They miscarried that baby ball, folks, and this game is over. What a disappointment for team Sexton."

That's one way to look at it. I suppose we could call it embryonic suicide but that implies that the baby took a good look around and thought, "This place sucks. I'm outta here!" before jumping ship. Then you're left calling after him, "Well, I would've cleaned up a little if I'd known you were coming."

Sigh.

Or we could call it exactly what it is: all the possibility of a baby wrapped up in your arms reduced to a mess of blood, clotted tissue, and tears. But that's a lot to write on a medical chart and would probably cause our would-be sympathizers to wince instead of offering the more appropriate pity face and hushed apologies.

So, miscarriage it is. And a miscarriage it was.

Just a week ago, Tim and I stood in the bathroom staring in disbelief at the bright blue plus sign in the tiny window of a pregnancy test. Needless to say we were shocked. SHOCKED! There were a couple of "what the fucks" and a "you're joking, right?" as well as several outbreaks of laughter. You know, the kind of laughter you might hear while walking through a mental hospital from some soul teetering between reality and insanity.

Tm shifted from side to side and front to back making sure that every angle revealed the same result. Positive. Positive. And positive. At thirty-nine and forty years old, we, infertile Tim and Amie, who had this very week sent our youngest to kindergarten, would be starting over again? From scratch? (That would be a "WTF?" spot right there.) But with the initial surprise over, it didn't take long to get excited.

We decided not to share until I could see the OB/GYN. Instead, we shot each other looks across the dinner table and had quiet conversations in the dark about things like hospitals and delivery rooms. Strange and surreal conversations that we had never had before. Not in nineteen years of marriage. Then, three days later, everything changed.

Around mid-morning, I noticed a strange burning sensation in my abdomen and I began to bleed. Not much at first, and we tried not to panic, but then the cramping started. The more severe the cramping, the greater the flow. By late afternoon, I was having trouble standing without doubling over so I basically camped out in the bathroom while Tim ran interference with the other children now home from school.

I considered calling the doctor but knew there was nothing could stop the inevitable. So I waited. Waited for confirmation. Waited for closure. Maybe I was just waiting for something to assure me that I hadn't imagined it all, that it really was me with a positive pregnancy test, that it really was us who'd been surprised and silly and giddy. Confirmation came. It was nothing recognizable, but still painfully obvious. I know that there are women who've suffered much more visually horrifying miscarriages or still births than this was. And while my worldview doesn't press me to grieve a baby in a viable sense, the death of potential - the baby I had carried to completion in my mind's eye - was no less heartrending.

Tim and I held each other and cried. We wiped our eyes and tucked our little ones into bed and then cried some more. We sucked it up, said goodnight to the other three kiddos, then met on the couch and cried some more. Then we dragged ourselves to bed and cried some more.

The days since have been difficult, including a hospital visit, ultrasounds of a very tender and woefully empty uterus, more abdominal cramping, sore boobs – all those things reminding me that my body is returning to "normal" and that I am not pregnant, in case for a single moment I have forgotten. Which, of course, I haven't. And every now and then I pull a pregnancy test out of my panty drawer and look at that blue plus sign. And then I look at the hospital discharge papers which read "Diagnosis: Complete Miscarriage" and I wonder whose life is this that I am watching and why does it feel so very real?

We didn't share that we were pregnant for two reasons. First, we knew that miscarriages can happen in early pregnancy and while it was hard being alone, we certainly didn't want to drag our already traumatized children along for the ride.

Secondly, we didn't want to hear it. You know exactly what I'm talking about. We didn't want to hear how "God is trying to get your attention" and "God is answering your prayer for a sign." And then, of course would have come the subsequent backpedaling when we had to spread the news of the miscarriage. The God who was intimately working to show himself to me would have suddenly been given a free pass on the train of "these things just sometimes happen." Oh, how we like to have our cake and eat it, too.

Here's the ugly truth, and I do mean ugly. *If* things I've said about God up to this point have not offended you (even though that's not my goal), you may want to take a deep breath before continuing because I will not pull any punches here. Ready? Need another second? Okay, it will no doubt be one hell of a run-on sentence but here goes:

If this was God, then it was a God who ignored my desire for having a biological child for several years, ignored my willingness to have a biological child for several more years, and ignored my direct plea for supernatural evidence of himself which could *easily* have included an unexpected pregnancy for several months, only to open my womb at the time of my life when I was absolutely content to watch my five children grow up and considering myself past the age of parenting small people, and then allowed me just enough time to not only accept but to rejoice in the idea of starting over, only to take that very child from me. *If this was God, he is one mean son-of-a-bitch.*

And frankly, if you are okay with this version of God (and remember, you can't have it both ways – either God opens and closes the womb or he doesn't) then you just might be a mean son-of-a-bitch, too.

I grieved hard over this pregnancy. Married almost twenty years and becoming pregnant for the first time at thirty-nine years old, who wouldn't? But I grieved differently, and that is why I included this section. Christians like to think they have the corner market on good grieving with that whole "we do not grieve as those who have no hope" thing, but I sincerely believe that science allowed me to process my situation and my grief with tremendous understanding and hope.

On a basic biological level, I can tell you why I likely got pregnant at this stage of life. Women often release more eggs per ovulation cycle as they near the age of menopause, the body's last-ditch effort to get those genes reproduced. The possibility of being pregnant with multiples increases for the same reason. And why the miscarriage? Could be any number of reasons on a cellular level, but I suspect it's because I have severe endometriosis. It doesn't mean that it's impossible for me to get pregnant (obviously) or impossible to carry a child to term; my chances are just lesser because my womb is compromised.

I never had to wonder if I had done something wrong, physically or spiritually. I never wondered if there was some greater lesson I was supposed to learn. There was no one I was obligated to be grateful to despite my sorrow. There was no one I had to be faithful to except myself and my experience. And there was sure as hell, no one I had to make excuses for.

Again, this miscarriage was devastating, but in some ways easier than losing Journey had been because I never tormented myself with visions of spiritual realms being shifted for or against me. There was just this life, and this life's incredible potential to create life and diversity, even if that diversity yields its own limitations for creating more life.

The Santa Claus Effect

>"**You sit on a throne of lies!**"
>-Buddy the Elf, *Elf*

We have been asked by some if we ever really believed it. Often it's presented more as an accusation than a question, but still. And pondering this idea one day, it hit me: the true answer to that question. I didn't walk away from Christianity because I didn't believe it enough. I walked away because I believed it *too* much.

Let me try to explain what I mean.

Did you do "Santa Claus" growing up? Maybe not. But I did. My family did. And I mean, we were all in. I remember sitting by the picture window in my grandmother's house on Christmas Eve watching the sky for that tiny blinking red-nosed reindeer. Surely I could see it because the news anchor had just reported that he'd been spotted over the Atlanta area. Soon, we would rush home to unload our loot from family and change into our jammies. Mom would always start a roaring fire in the fireplace and I would immediately begin to worry. *How would Santa make it in safely if she insisted on scorching him to death?* But my parents assured me that the fire would die down in time and that Santa always had elves who could pick the door locks in case he needed a backup plan.

I adored Santa. Never mind that he'd all but ignored my letters requesting a puppy in my stocking EVERY SINGLE

YEAR. He probably just didn't want to make my parents mad because they certainly didn't want me to have one. I just loved him and I believed in him. And I knew that not believing in him would really, really hurt his feelings, and I never wanted to hurt Santa's feelings.

I started to get a little older and started to have some suspicions about Old Saint Nick. There seemed to be so many things that didn't quite add up. He claimed to do things that sounded just plain impossible and I'd certainly never witnessed this "magic" of his. I kept running into this brick wall of logic and reality, but he was jolly and loving and most of all, dependent upon my belief to continue his good work. So, year after year, I propped up my belief with more explanations and more excuses because believing was most important. Until I was around eight years old, and the curtain fell.

It wasn't actually Christmas. It was the Saturday before Easter and my mom told dad to stop off at the store and keep us kids in the car while she ran in for just a few groceries. No biggie. She hopped back into the car and tossed her bags onto the floorboard by her feet. And that's when I spotted it. The yellow packaging. The brown writing. And the strangely fuzzy textured treat inside. Peeps. Mom bought Peeps. The same kind of Peeps that were always in our Easter basket. The Easter basket that the *Easter Bunny* filled with goodies. Suddenly, there was no denying the truth. No excuse would suffice. There was no pulling a rabbit out of a hat. There was nothing else I could do to perpetuate the fantasy.

"Mom, are you the Easter Bunny?" I asked from the back seat.

She didn't answer right away but it wasn't necessary. I knew. And then suddenly, my world was spinning. I gasped. "Does that mean you and Daddy are Santa Claus, too?"

I remember that she patted my dad's stomach and said something related to a jolly, old, fat guy. As I said in the beginning of this book, I was an emotionally sensitive kid. I think this plays into my capacity for memories because they are so deeply rooted with feelings, and I can tell you exactly how I felt riding home with the windows down on that beautiful spring day. I wanted to cry because I was so deeply disappointed. I felt foolish for all the ways I'd defending him against bigger kids who knew the truth all along.

And I felt totally relieved.

Stories that never made sense no longer needed to make sense. Questions that had no answers no longer needed answers. Magical impossibilities no longer needed to be possible. Unfulfilled wishes no longer needed a higher purpose. You see I hadn't believed in Santa too *little*. I had believed in him too *much*. And that is why I had to stop believing.

I can also tell you exactly how I felt the day I stopped believing in God. I cried because I was so deeply disappointed. I felt foolish for all the ways I'd defended him. And I felt totally relieved. I never believed in God too little. I believed in him too much. And that is why I had to stop believing.

Getting a Foothold

> **"The still faithful might say I never truly knew grace, never had it; but they would be wrong. The truth is that I found it and abandoned it…My heart continued to believe in the light and the way, but increasing in the abstract, and I looked for grace in some other setting…I was enchanted with science as a means of explaining the physical world, which increasingly seemed to me to be the complete world.**
>
> **In essence, I still longed for grace but rooted solidly on Earth."**
>   **-Edward O. Wilson, *Naturalist***

I was sitting at the table one day, feeling a bit weighed down by the path my life had taken when my then four year-old started this random conversation with me:

  Justus: Mom, God gives you all of the food, and all of your children.

  Me: Okay.

Justus: And the rain and sun that makes the plants grow. He gives you everything.

Me: Where is God, Justus?

Justus: In the sky.

Me: What does he want from us?

Justus: Nothing, mom. He doesn't want anything from us.

Could it really be that simple? Could it really be that God wants nothing from us? Not proper worship, not glory, not even relationship per se. Could it be that "god" would be satisfied by the simple recognition of our connection, the ability and human obligation to uplift souls even as our soul needs to be uplifted? Maybe that *is* the goal. Maybe that is the goal apart from the existence of *any* god.

I would've liked to have added a Part Six: Back on the Mountain Top section. Something that says, "Hey, look how we've made it out of the crap and now we're better than ever!" Sometimes I totally feel that way. I could dance and sing and shout because the freedom is so tangible. But that's not really the way life works, is it? I mean, mountains are impressive because they are few and far between. It's the monotonous terrain of valleys and plateaus that drives us to look up in awe and wonder. Which means that most days we're just struggling to pay the bills, working out this crazy parenting gig, and doing our best to connect with each other on a level deeper than just "did you feed the dog?" In a nutshell, nothing has changed. Life is life and in the end, religion isn't much more than who you give lip service to while you do your life just like everyone else is doing theirs; it's the credits rolling at the end of the movie.

And so, I haven't created a new religion. Never intended to. I haven't adequately destroyed old religion. Never thought I could. I've just tried to share my journey, the how and why of it and where I think it's leading, for now. If anything, I took the religion I grew up with and simultaneously narrowed it to one principal while expanding it to encompass a global community.

I'm not a staunch atheist as far as atheism goes. I leave room for lots of question marks. I'm not a Christian as far as Christianity goes. I leave room for *too many* question marks. And I'm probably not even a very good agnostic. But having spent so many years seeing people in categories of "saved or lost," "sheep or goats," "wheat or tares," "in or out," I'm pretty sick of all that labeling anyway.

Still, having lived the Christian life for so long, I know that labeling is part of the system. I can quote, have memorized, and have used at some point, all of the standard arguments.

When I share the things we've done in obedience to Christ, I know that one eyebrow will go up and you will think *aha, works based salvation!* But you're wrong. We knew grace. We lived grace. We lived salvation by grace. We lived and preached obedience as a response to salvation, *not* as a means for obtaining salvation.

When I share the things that have hurt us and the people who have disappointed us, I know that you will shake your head and think *aha, they are just battle sore and wounded by the church.* But you're wrong. Our loyalty was built on that battlefield and every scrape came while fighting for the integrity of Christ's bride and trying to dig deeper into the Word.

When I share the ways we have tested the Scripture and found it lacking, and of the promises which sound good on paper but have built-in escape clauses and never really see fruition, I know that your lip will curl into a half smile and you will think *aha, they think they know it all. They are just prideful and arrogant!* But you're wrong. We were most humbled when we realized that everything we "knew" amounted to nothing.

Aha, they were never really saved!

Aha, they read too many books!

Aha, they didn't read the right books!

Aha, they didn't read the Bible enough.

Aha, they read the Bible too much and took it too literally!

Aha, aha, aha!

I know the boxes so very well.

One of the saddest moments in all of our twenty years of ministry came on the heels of our departure from the small church in central Georgia. A church member/choir member/woman-who-helped-us-purchase-our-first-home-

and-eventually-resell-that-same-home/friend, stood on my porch step and said, "I love you and Tim and I know because of the kind of people you are that whatever happened to cause you to leave the church must have been really, really bad. But please don't tell me because *I am too old and set in my routine to have to change churches now*."

I fear this is where too many people reside. And I understand from the depths of my being the desire to maintain comfort over knowledge, to cling to that which is familiar because flying without a net is just so scary.

If you've read this book, you may have already felt some pangs of discomfort and for your willingness to endure those I am very grateful. If you could avoid the instinct to try and draw those four corners around us I would be even more grateful. I know that I haven't answered every question or addressed every argument. I know that most arguments are purely subjective and therefore unanswerable. I only hoped that you would see past the labels of religion, the categories, the boxes, and realize that there is a person. Under the label of Christian, there was me. And in most ways my reflection of Christianity, my interpretation of it, were really just reflections of me. Likewise under the label of agnostic, apostate, unbeliever, whatever you choose, there is me and the reflections of me.

Did you like me before? Why? Because I was a Christian? *Only* because I was a Christian? In that case, I understand if your friendship is among those that we have lost or which have been terribly strained. But if you liked me because I was funny, kind, friendly, sarcastic, witty, goofy, honest, clumsy, or passionate, I am happy to tell you that the person you liked is still here.

I am still here.

And for me, it comes down to this: I could spend the rest of my life trying to convince myself and others that a book written two thousand years ago does or does not say what it does or does not say. Sigh. I could spend the rest of my life trying to figure out if another holy book written by other holy men dictated by a different holy god is more palatable. Holy headache Batman!

Or instead I *could* (and I will) simply spend the rest of my life being as fully human as humanly possible. I will keep my feet rooted firmly in the earth. I may occasionally still long for grace, but mostly, I will just live and love, here and now.

I hope that whatever faith, religion, or belief system you subject yourself to will allow you to do the same.

Made in the USA
Columbia, SC
03 April 2024